P9-CAE-725

USING ENGLISH
GRAMMAR AND WRITING SKILLS

SECOND COURSE

ADRIAN B. SANFORD

CENTER FOR THE STUDY OF INSTRUCTION
San Francisco

HARCOURT BRACE JOVANOVICH
New York Chicago San Francisco Atlanta Dallas *and* London

THE AUTHOR

ADRIAN B. SANFORD has taught English for more than a quarter of a century. He has also written materials for English instruction and conducted workshops for educators.

CONSULTING EDUCATORS AND TEACHERS

ENNO KLAMMER
Eastern Oregon State College
La Grande, Oregon

MARIAN O. JENKINS
Coral Springs High School
Coral Springs, Florida

JO ANN STEWART
Lowell High School
San Francisco, California

ROBERT LEON
Palo Alto High School
Palo Alto, California

KEITH CALDWELL
Kennedy High School
Fremont, California

KEITH WILL
San Juan Unified School District
Carmichael, California

CYNTHIA BAKER
Starr King Intermediate
Carmichael, California

JACK STRANGE
Arcade Intermediate
Carmichael, California

BARBARA S. DEAN
Will Rogers School
Fair Oaks, California

SYBILLE IRWIN
Winston Churchill Intermediate
Carmichael, California

JUDY A. KANTER
Howe Avenue Intermediate
Sacramento, California

BARBARA COULTER
Louis Pasteur School
Orangeville, California

ACKNOWLEDGMENTS

The publisher gratefully acknowledges the contributions of Jo Ann Stewart and Charlotte Herbert to the preparation of the Review Exercises for the series.

For permission to reprint copyrighted material, grateful acknowledgment is made to the following sources:

Harcourt Brace Jovanovich, Inc.: From *The HBJ School Dictionary*, copyright © 1977.

The H. W. Wilson Company: From *The Readers' Guide to Periodical Literature*, June 10, 1977, copyright © 1977.

Harper & Row, Publishers, Inc.: Excerpt from *The Adventures of Tom Sawyer* by Mark Twain.

DIANA WHITELEY
Project Editor

PATRICIA HOSLEY
Editor

SALLY THOMPSON
Text Designer

Printed in the United States of America

ISBN 0-15-311701-X

TO THE STUDENT

As you begin using this book, take time to become familiar with its special features. Notice the organization of sections and chapters of the book as shown in the Contents. Look within a chapter to see how the rules and definitions are printed. Note the use of color and special type to highlight important points.

An alphabetized index in the back of the book lists all the important topics in the textbook, with their page numbers. The colored tabs at the corners of the pages allow you to find any topic by its chapter number. The glossary in the back of the book gives an alphabetical listing of special terms in English. Each is followed by a definition. Many of the terms have examples to illustrate their meaning or use.

On certain pages you can see cross references printed in the margins. These refer you to other parts of the textbook where you can find additional information.

These features—and more—have been built into the book to aid you.

From this textbook you can learn a great deal about how to improve your use of English. Improvement, however, requires that you apply yourself to studying the textbook and to using what you can learn from it. As either a book assigned by your teacher or a reference tool in which you find what you need, this book offers you the opportunity to grow stronger in using English.

A.B.S.

CONTENTS

CHAPTER

1

PARTS OF SPEECH

Nouns, Pronouns, Adjectives

The different words people use work in different ways to help carry meaning. Some words name people or things. Other words tell of actions or tell what the people or things look like. Still other words tell how the actions are carried out. There are eight different kinds of words used to carry meaning.

The eight different kinds of words are called the parts of speech: *nouns, pronouns, adjectives, verbs, adverbs, prepositions, conjunctions,* and *interjections.* Chapters 1 and 2 deal with these eight parts of speech.

NOUNS

1a A noun is a word or a group of words used to name someone or something.

A noun may name a living thing.

EXAMPLES people, animals, vegetable, Pedro, Ellen, nurses, Dr. Kimura, Tabby, snails, plums, fish, cow, Lassie, son-in-law, whales, actor

A noun may name a thing that is not living.

EXAMPLES apartment, baseballs, chair, valleys, wind, London Bridge, magazines, lamp, hill, wall

A noun may name a place.

EXAMPLES Toledo, New York, Alaska, school, park, Midtown Theater, Lion's Restaurant

A noun may name an action.

EXAMPLES dancing, work, arguing, walking, wrestling, attempt, drawing, act

A noun may name an idea.

EXAMPLES beauty, democracy, good, truth, friendship, justice, freedom

A noun may name a season or a period of time.

EXAMPLES fall, summer, afternoon, week, Monday, 3:30 P.M., noon

Any word used to name something is a noun.

EXERCISE 1 Number a sheet of paper 1–10. After each number write the nouns that appear in each sentence.

EXAMPLE The creatures of Africa have interested humans for years.

creatures, Africa, humans, years

1. Many animals live in the jungles and rivers of Africa.
2. Hippos and crocodiles live in the waters of Africa.
3. Fish, snakes, birds, frogs, and turtles also live on that continent.
4. One snake was over four meters long.
5. Gorillas live in the mountains.
6. People have studied these animals.
7. Observers have spent winter, spring, and summer watching the families of gorillas.
8. The gorillas make sounds like burping and grunting.
9. These noises express happiness and anger.
10. If a gorilla ever grunts near you, put on a big smile.

Common Nouns and Proper Nouns

(1) Common nouns name kinds of persons, places, or things. Proper nouns name particular persons, places, or things.

Every proper noun begins with a capital letter. See Capitalization, p. 197

EXAMPLES

COMMON NOUNS	PROPER NOUNS
girl	Alice
city	Detroit
elephant	Jumbo
state	California

Sometimes a proper noun may be made up of more than one word. If a proper noun is made up of more than one word, each important word is capitalized.

EXAMPLES Tom Jones, Hee Jung Lee, Dr. Andrews, Central Park, First State Bank of Illinois

EXERCISE 2 Number a sheet of paper 1–10. After each number, list the proper nouns in the sentence.

EXAMPLE Tom and Marion both read *The Red Pony.*

Tom, Marion, The Red Pony

1. People used to think that Martians might live on Mars.
2. H. G. Wells, a writer in England, wrote a famous book about an invasion from Mars.
3. *The War of the Worlds* was made into a radio play broadcast by CBS in 1938.
4. Orson Welles produced the play that was heard in America.
5. It was broadcast in October just in time for Halloween.
6. In the play a spaceship landed near Trenton, New Jersey.
7. Professor Pierson from Princeton University arrived with the New Jersey State Police at the scene.
8. The play told how the invading Martians killed police, citizens, and soldiers who belonged to the National Guard.

9. Some listeners thought invaders from Mars actually had landed.
10. The police in New York and New Jersey received many calls.

Singular Nouns and Plural Nouns

1b A noun may be singular or plural.

A noun may name one thing. It is called a *singular noun.*

EXAMPLES house, dance, dancer, apple, boy, woman

A noun may name more than one thing. It is called a *plural noun.*

EXAMPLES houses, dances, dancers, apples, boys, women

Most singular nouns add the letter **s** to form their plurals.

EXAMPLES dog/dogs, place/places

EXERCISE 3 The following nouns are all singular. Number a sheet of paper 1–10. Rewrite each noun to make it plural.

EXAMPLE table

tables

1. pie
2. slice
3. mirror
4. hamburger
5. pizza
6. tiger
7. snail
8. pin
9. car
10. answer

Singular nouns that end in the letters **s, x, ch, sh,** and **z** are made into plural nouns by adding the letters **es.**

EXAMPLES stress/stress**es**, bus/bus**es**, wax/wax**es**, switch/switch**es**, marsh/marsh**es**, quiz/quiz**zes**

Note that some nouns double the **z** before adding **es.**

Singular nouns that end in a consonant + **y** form their plurals this way: the **y** is changed to **i.** Then **es** is added.

EXAMPLES navy = nav**i** + **es** = navies
pantry = pant**ri** + **es** = pantries

Other singular nouns ending in **y** add **s** to form their plurals.

EXAMPLES toy/toy**s**, play/play**s**

EXERCISE 4 Number a sheet of paper 1–10. Some of the following nouns are singular. Others are plural. Rewrite each noun. Make the singular nouns plural and the plural nouns singular.

EXAMPLE treaty

treaties

1. watch
2. church
3. tray
4. dairies
5. boxes
6. witches
7. army
8. whizzes
9. waltz
10. sixes

Possessive Nouns

1c A noun can show that something else belongs to it or is related to it.

When a noun shows that something belongs to it or is related to it, the noun is in the *possessive case.*

See Case, p. 313

EXAMPLES Wilma's shoes, the boy's kite, Mother's cat, Elaine's record, sun's light, the school's team

The possessive case of most singular nouns is made by adding an apostrophe (') and the letter **s**.

EXAMPLES dog**'s** growl, person**'s** choice, cat**'s** meow, Juanita**'s** friend

The possessive case of a plural noun ending in **s** is made by adding only an apostrophe.

EXAMPLES tigers**'** lair, wolves**'** howls, workers**'** party

The possessive case of a plural noun that does not end in **s** is made by adding an apostrophe and an **s**.

EXAMPLES men**'s** arguments, children**'s** scores, oxen**'s** yokes, women**'s** magazines

EXERCISE 5 Here are ten nouns. Use each in its possessive form in a sentence of your own. You should have ten sentences.

1. dog
2. crowd
3. trucks
4. lions
5. men
6. Francisco
7. sandwich
8. cats
9. ox
10. clubs

Compound Nouns

A noun may be made up of two or more words used together to name someone or something. This kind of a noun is called a *compound noun.*

EXAMPLES football
father-in-law

Many compound words are written as one word.

EXAMPLES chalkboard
bedroom
downbeat

Some are written with a hyphen.

EXAMPLES make-up
change-over

A few are written as separate words.

EXAMPLES attorney general
fire alarm
Great Britain

If you are unsure of the form of a compound noun, check a dictionary.

PRONOUNS

1d A pronoun is a word used to take the place of a noun or a noun word group.

EXAMPLES *Marion* called to *Jim and me.*
She called to *us.*

The first six prisoners marched away.
They marched away.

In the first pair of sentences above, the pronoun *she* stands for the proper noun *Marion.* The pronoun *us* stands for the group of words *Jim and me.* In the second pair of sentences, the pronoun *they* stands for the noun word group *the first six prisoners.*

Here are more examples of pronouns that take the place of nouns and noun word groups.

The first cars rode over *the bridge.*
They rode over *it.*

Judy and Maurie gave the answer to *Sharon.*
They gave the answer to *her.*

Ken and I want to go with *Dominic and Donna.*
We want to go with *them.*

Here is a list of pronouns. Next to each pronoun are things the pronoun can stand for.

I	(the person speaking)
you	(the person spoken to)
he	Dave Dumpy, boy
she	Nancy Gonzales, female
it	an object, idea, or animal

we	all of us together
you	all of you together
they	Dave and Nancy

EXERCISE 6 Number a sheet of paper 1–6. Each of the following sentences has one or more pronouns in it. After each number write the pronouns in the sentence.

EXAMPLE Many Americans have heard of the battle of the Alamo, but they do not all know what it stands for.

they, it

1. *Alamo* in Spanish is the name for the cottonwood tree, but it also names a famous fort in San Antonio, Texas.
2. The last battle for the Alamo took place in 1836 before you and I were born.
3. General Santa Anna led the Mexican troops to victory, but they suffered heavy losses.
4. Jim Bowie was in the final fight, but he did not win it.
5. He is famous for a long knife called the bowie knife.
6. Davy Crockett was with the two hundred people in the Alamo, and together they fought to the death to defend it.

Personal Pronouns

1e A personal pronoun stands for a noun or noun word group that names a person, place, or thing.

EXAMPLES Jim gave a snapshot to Marcia.
He gave *it* to *her.*

The little picture showed Jim on a horse.
It showed Jim on a horse.

Here is a list of personal pronouns.

SINGULAR	PLURAL
I, me, my, mine	we, us, our, ours
you, your, yours	you, your, yours
he, him, his she, her, hers it, its	they, them, their, theirs

(1) The subjective case of a personal pronoun shows the person, place, or thing being talked about.

The following personal pronouns are in the *subjective case:*

SINGULAR	PLURAL
I	we
you	you
he she it	they

A pronoun in the *subjective case* can take the place of a noun that acts or is told about in a sentence.

(2) The objective case of a personal pronoun shows the object or result of something that happens.

The following personal pronouns are in the *objective case:*

SINGULAR	PLURAL
me	us
you	you
him, her, it	them

EXERCISE 7 Each of the following sentences has a personal pronoun in the subjective case in parentheses following it. Rewrite each sentence. Take out the underlined words. Put in the personal pronoun in the objective case.

EXAMPLE Give Toby the hat I made for Toby. (he)

Give Toby the hat I made for him.

1. Alice looked at the mirror, then stepped through the mirror. (it)
2. Alice met a man with a hat who asked Alice to tea. (she)
3. Because the hatter said strange things, everyone called the hatter the Mad Hatter. (he)
4. Other strange guests were at tea so that she had a chance to meet the other guests. (they)
5. Sometimes they were not polite to Alice. (she)

(3) The possessive case of a personal pronoun shows that something belongs to someone or something.

Here is a list of pronouns in the *possessive case.*

SINGULAR	PLURAL
my, mine	our, ours
your, yours	your, yours
his, her, hers, its	their, theirs

The possessive pronouns *my, your, his, her, its, our,* and *their* are used before nouns. Examples are *See my house* and *Give them their tickets.* These pronouns may also be called *possessive adjectives.*

See Adjective, p. 311

EXERCISE 8 Each of the following sentences has a blank in it and a personal pronoun in parentheses following it. Rewrite each sentence. Put in the possessive case of the pronoun.

EXAMPLE The human body has bones inside ______ flesh. (it)

The human body has bones inside its flesh.

1. The bones of ______ body are called a skeleton. (you)
2. Both men and women have the same number of bones in ______ skeletons. (they)
3. Your body has 206 bones, and so does ______. (I)
4. My bones look the same as ______. (you)
5. Your smallest bone is part of ______ ear. (you)
6. My largest bone is ______ thigh bone. (I)
7. When you are young, ______ bones are softer. (you)

8. Old people find ______ bones get brittle. (they)
9. Your body could not stand without ______ skeleton. (it)
10. If all people have ______ own bones, why does a skeleton scare some people? (they)

ADJECTIVES

1f An adjective is a word used to modify or describe a noun or a pronoun.

Use an adjective to tell *what kind, which one, how much,* or *how many.*

EXAMPLES		
	what kind	a *happy* person
		a *good* friend
	which one	the *larger* car
		the *slowest* turtle
	how many or how much	*five* pieces
		several reasons

The words *a, an,* and *the* are special adjectives called *articles.* You will probably find at least one article in every sentence you read, write, or speak.

EXERCISE 9 Copy the following sentences. Underline the adjectives. Draw an arrow from each adjective to the word it describes. Do not underline the articles *a, an,* and *the.*

EXAMPLE That is a funny magazine.

That is a funny magazine.

1. People like to eat sweet foods.
2. An important sweetener is sugar.
3. Sugar comes from a tall cane that grows in hot climates.
4. It also comes from a fat beet.
5. The sweet cane looks like high grass.
6. It has thick stalks filled with rich juice.
7. The stalks are cut and then squeezed in a strong crusher.
8. This releases a brown liquid that is cooked in large vats.
9. The muddy liquid turns into a thick syrup.
10. The heavy syrup forms into dry crystals.
11. The crystals are refined to make brown sugar and white sugar.
12. The sugar is put into large packages or small boxes and sold to people who have a "sweet tooth."

EXERCISE 10 Number a sheet of paper 1–12. List the adjectives in each sentence.

EXAMPLE Beets for sugar are grown on large farms.

large

1. This is a short story about what happened to little seeds, fat beets, and candy.
2. The beets started as tiny seeds.

3. An old farmer in sunny California planted the seeds in his field.
4. He dug a shallow trench in the soft earth.
5. Then he put in the dry seeds and covered them with rich soil.
6. He wet them with water taken from the long canal near the farm.
7. The hot sun helped the seeds sprout green leaves.
8. Later he dug up the grey beets.
9. He sold them to a huge factory where they were turned into white sugar.
10. The sweet crystals were packed and shipped to a small factory.
11. There they were made into red gumdrops and green lollipops.
12. Later the old farmer bought some and gave them to four young grandchildren.

An adjective usually comes in front of the noun it modifies. Sometimes it comes later in a sentence. When it comes later, it may be called an *adjective completer* because it completes the description of an earlier noun or pronoun.

See Sentences, pp. 86–87

EXAMPLE Rosanna is *friendly.*

EXERCISE 11 Following is a list of twenty words. Ten of those words are adjectives. Use each of the ten adjectives to fill the ten blanks in the sentences beneath the list. Write the words on your own paper.

EXAMPLE The boy is ______.

cold

cold	true	angry	tired
shadow	very	sometimes	small
of	because	onto	yet
pleased	walks	happy	beautiful
hold	young	wet	bet

1. The ______ dog shivered.
2. The ______ girl fell asleep.
3. The package was quite ______.
4. They seem ______.
5. The ______ children laughed at her jokes.
6. They got out of their ______ clothes.
7. I think that is ______.
8. Several ______ birds landed there.
9. The puppy was very ______.
10. His parents were ______.

Comparison of Adjectives

1g An adjective may change form to show how one thing compares with another.

The adjectives you have studied so far are in the *positive* form. Nearly all adjectives change form to show how something compares with something else.

Most adjectives add **er** to show comparison. This form is called the *comparative*.

EXAMPLES My radio is *small.* (positive form)
It is *smaller* than your radio. (comparative form)

To show comparison of three or more things, most adjectives add **est.** This is called the *superlative* form.

EXAMPLES The Whammy plays *loud* music. (positive form)
The Whammy plays *louder* music. (comparative form)
The Whammy plays the *loudest* music in the place. (superlative form)

Long adjectives usually do not add **er** or **est** to form the comparative or superlative. Instead, they add *more* or *most* in front of the positive form.

EXAMPLES

POSITIVE
wonderful
graceful
useful

COMPARATIVE
more wonderful
more graceful
more useful

SUPERLATIVE
most wonderful
most graceful
most useful

Irregular Adjectives

Some adjectives are irregular. They are called irregular because they do not add **er** or **est** as most adjectives do. Following is a list of the most common irregular adjectives.

POSITIVE	COMPARATIVE	SUPERLATIVE
bad	worse	worst
good	better	best
many	more	most
little	less	least
old	older (elder)	oldest (eldest)
far	farther (further)	farthest (furthest)

EXERCISE 12 Number a sheet of paper 1–10. Write the correct form of the adjective that belongs in the blank in each sentence.

EXAMPLES He has ______ money than Barry. (little)

less

Tamara is ______ than Shalene. (ambitious)

more ambitious

1. Many people think San Francisco is the ______ city they have ever seen in the United States. (colorful)
2. Its hills are ______ than those of any other major city in California. (high)
3. Visitors exclaim that its views are ______ than they have seen in any city. (spectacular)
4. It has one of the ______ climates of any city in the nation. (good)
5. Its ______ temperature in the summer is rarely more than 32° Celsius. (warm)
6. In the winter its ______ days stay above the freezing level. (cold)

7. It has some of the ______ hotels found anywhere in the world. (elegant)
8. Its best restaurants serve some of the ______ meals you can eat. (delicious)
9. But a visit to San Francisco costs ______ dollars than I have. (many)
10. I guess it will be ______ to stay home than to take that trip. (cheap)

REVIEW EXERCISE A Common and Proper Nouns

Make two lists on a sheet of paper. Label one list *Common Nouns*. Label the other list *Proper Nouns*. Write the nouns from the following paragraphs in the correct lists. Do not list dates.

The first colonies of North America were founded in the seventeenth century. King James of England granted charters to groups of people who wanted to live there. A region called Virginia was settled first. Next came a colony near the Kennebec River, now a part of Maine. Its settlers gave up their homes after a bad winter in 1608.

By 1620 the Puritans had come by way of Holland to settle near Cape Cod. Their land later became a part of Massachusetts.

Other people settled along the East Coast of the continent. It took more than one hundred years for Georgia to become the thirteenth colony.

REVIEW EXERCISE B Plurals

Number a sheet of paper 1–12. Next to each number write the plural form of each of the following words.

EXAMPLE button

buttons

1. light
2. dash
3. trick
4. turkey
5. thief
6. half
7. puppy
8. valley
9. echo
10. lady
11. buzz
12. stitch

REVIEW EXERCISE C Possessive Forms

Number a sheet of paper 1–12. Next to each number write the possessive form of each word.

EXAMPLE José

José's

1. man
2. children
3. monkey
4. table
5. sisters
6. watch
7. trees
8. house
9. glass
10. donkeys
11. women
12. Skippy

REVIEW EXERCISE D **Pronouns**

Write the following sentences on a sheet of paper. Replace each underlined word or group of words with one of these pronouns.

he	them	his
it	her	its
they	him	

EXAMPLE Lucy Manon has braces on Lucy Manon's teeth.

Lucy Manon has braces on her teeth.

1. When a tug boat captain saw a dog swimming in the Pacific Ocean, the tug boat captain was curious.
2. The captain's boat went toward the brave dog.
3. The captain remembered the famous swimmers Esther Williams and Mark Spitz and thought he might name the dog for Esther Williams or Mark Spitz.
4. Of course, the captain admired the dog and wanted to help the dog.
5. The captain threw the dog a life raft which the dog was very glad to climb aboard.
6. Now the dog has the dog's own tug boat.
7. The captain has made a comfortable place for the dog in his cabin where the dog and the master can be together out of bad weather.
8. The dog is too comfortable and happy with its master and its boat to leave its master and its boat for the cold sea.

REVIEW EXERCISE E Pronouns

Number a sheet of paper 1–8. Choose the correct pronoun from the list for the blank in each sentence and write it on your paper. You may use a pronoun more than once.

his	it	them
their	him	he
its		

EXAMPLE Captain John Smith sailed ______ ship from England.

his

1. Captain John Smith took ______ men sailing up the coast of North America in 1614.
2. He sailed to New England, which was named by ______.
3. Then, without settling there, ______ and his men sailed south.
4. Almost ten years later the Puritans sailed in ______ ships to settle Gloucester, Massachusetts.
5. By 1636, some of ______ had moved to establish homes in Connecticut and Rhode Island.
6. New York had ______ beginning when the Dutch settled along the Hudson River in the 1620's.
7. Owners of land in the Carolinas founded a settlement in 1670 and called ______ Charles Town.
8. Many Quakers made ______ homes in Pennsylvania, New Jersey, and Delaware.

REVIEW EXERCISE F Adjectives

Write the following sentences on a sheet of paper. Skip a line between the sentences. Underline each adjective. Do not underline articles. Draw an arrow from each adjective to the noun or the pronoun that it modifies.

EXAMPLE The small town of Salem, Massachusetts, became the center of evil stories in 1692.

The small town of Salem, Massachusetts, became the center of evil stories in 1692.

1. The colonists believed in mysterious witchcraft.
2. They thought that certain people possessed strange powers.
3. The unusual powers came from an unearthly source.
4. The powers could bring bad luck to others.
5. Sensible people became unhappy because of the great fear of witches.
6. Innocent people were accused of evil deeds.
7. Some claimed these people had flown on old broomsticks when the moon was full.
8. Officials in Salem became afraid.
9. They tried the unlucky accused in a noisy court.
10. Before the year ended, hundreds of innocent people had been jailed and twenty unfortunate citizens had been hanged.

REVIEW EXERCISE G Nouns, Pronouns, Adjectives

Write the numbers 1–15 on a sheet of paper. After each number write the numbered word from the following paragraphs. Next to each word write *N* if it is a noun, *P* if it is a pronoun, or *A* if it is an adjective.

EXAMPLE *king, N.*

George III was the king[1] of England in 1763. When he[2] demanded large[3] taxes from the American colonies, he caused trouble. Americans believed the taxes were unfair[4]. The tax on tea[5] made them[6] very angry[7].

In 1773, a group of colonists in Boston[8] dressed up in costume[9]. Then they[10] rowed in boats out to a British ship in Boston harbor. The ship[11] was loaded with tea. The colonists dumped the tea into the harbor. This daring act angered the British. In fact, it[12] caused King George to close the port[13] of Boston.

The Boston Tea Party, as the event[14] was called later, became famous[15] throughout the colonies. It and other events led to the Revolutionary War.

REVIEW EXERCISE H Using Parts of Speech

Number a sheet of paper 1–8. After each number write a sentence in which you use the noun, pronoun, and adjective listed after that number in the following list. Underline each word that you use.

EXAMPLE

Bill his messy

Bill fled from his messy room.

	NOUNS	PRONOUNS	ADJECTIVES
1.	lion	it or its	smooth
2.	shoe	his or her	old
3.	sandwich	it or its	thick
4.	Theresa	she or her	stubborn
5.	Herbert	he or him	silly
6.	singer	his or her	beautiful
7.	siren	it or its	frightening
8.	neighbor	he or she	unfriendly

CHAPTER

2

PARTS OF SPEECH

Verbs, Adverbs, Prepositions, Conjunctions, Interjections

The parts of speech treated in this chapter are *verbs, adverbs, prepositions, conjunctions,* and *interjections*. Each works in its own way in a sentence. As you study these five parts of speech, you will increase your understanding of the grammar of the sentence.

VERBS

2a A verb is a word used to tell what happens or what exists.

EXAMPLES The clock *ticks*.
Its hands *move*.
We *are* late.

Two kinds of verbs are *action verbs* and *linking verbs*.

Action Verbs

(1) An action verb tells what someone or something does.

EXAMPLES Josh *sleeps* after lunch.
[*Sleeps* tells what Josh does.]

Abby *jogs* in the morning.
[*Jogs* tells what Abby does.]

Hiram *tripped* over his foot.
[*Tripped* tells what Hiram did.]

EXERCISE 1 Number a sheet of paper 1–12. Next to each number write the action verb in each sentence.

EXAMPLE Balloons float in the air.
float

1. Humans first successfully soared in a balloon in 1783.
2. Two Frenchmen made the first balloons out of cloth.
3. They built a small fire.
4. They then placed the open end of a large bag over the fire.
5. The hot air rose from the fire into the bag.
6. The air filled the bag.
7. The bag went almost out of sight.
8. The Frenchmen constructed a larger bag with a basket underneath.
9. They put a chicken, a goose, and a sheep in the basket.

10. The balloon carried the animals a little way up and safely down again.
11. Next, the Frenchmen tried this experiment with a man.
12. The successful experiment launched human exploration away from the earth.

Linking Verbs

(2) A linking verb expresses a state of being or links someone or something to words that complete its meaning.

A linking verb often begins a description about someone or something. The verb links or ties a person, place, or thing to other words that complete the description.

Here is a list of common linking verbs: *am, are, is, was, were, become, appear,* and *seems.*

EXAMPLES I *am* strong.
Willie *seems* tired.
She *was* early.

A linking verb is usually followed by another word that completes the meaning of the sentence. These words are called *completers.*

See Sentences, pp. 86–87

EXERCISE 2 Number a sheet of paper 1–8. Write the linking verb in each sentence next to its number.

EXAMPLE Tammie was shorter last year.

was

1. Children grow taller each year.
2. Last year Tammie was just over four feet tall.
3. She looked like a midget.
4. Her clothes were too large.
5. This year she is six inches taller.
6. She seems too big for her clothes.
7. I am almost big enough for them now.
8. Children become adults in time.

EXERCISE 3 Write five sentences. Use at least one action verb in each sentence and underline it.

EXERCISE 4 Write five sentences. Use at least one linking verb in each sentence and underline it.

Hint: Remember that a linking verb joins with another word or words to describe a person, place, or thing. An action verb tells of something that happens or has happened.

See Phrases, pp. 59–60

Action verbs and linking verbs do the main job of telling what someone did or what someone is like. They are *main verbs*. Sometimes main verbs have *helping verbs*. The main verb and its helping verb or verbs are called the *complete verb*, or *verb phrase*.

Helping Verbs

(3) A helping verb helps the main verb tell what happens or what exists.

Here are some common helping verbs: *was, were, can, could, have, should, will,* and *do.*

EXAMPLES Hyun Sook *could run* like a deer.
Nan *will arrive* in time for supper.

EXERCISE 5 Number a sheet of paper 1–8. Next to each number write the helping verb and the main verb in each sentence. Draw a line under each helping verb.

EXAMPLE Frogs can swim easily.

can swim

1. A frog had jumped into our pool one day.
2. It could float on the surface of the water.
3. I had touched its rounded nose a few times.
4. Every time, it would swim away under water.
5. My touch had frightened it.
6. The next day it had disappeared.
7. It had liked the water.
8. My actions had made it angry.

Tense

2b Most verbs change form to show a change in time.

The present time, called *present tense,* is usually shown by the *infinitive,* or base, form of a verb.

EXAMPLES You *live* on Tenth Avenue.
They *cook* doughnuts in the morning.

Most verbs show past time—the *simple past tense*—by adding **d** or **ed** to the infinitive form.

EXAMPLES You *lived* on Tenth Avenue.
They *cooked* doughnuts in the morning.

To show *future time,* most verbs use a helping verb with the infinitive form.

EXAMPLES You *will live* on Tenth Avenue.
They *will cook* doughnuts in the morning.

Here are more examples.

PRESENT I *work* hard.
PAST She *worked* hard.
FUTURE They *will work* hard.

PRESENT I *dance* poorly.
PAST We *danced* poorly.
FUTURE I *will dance* poorly.

PRESENT He *plays* a flute.
PAST You *played* a flute.
FUTURE I *will play* a flute.

The infinitive often takes the word *to* in front of it.

EXAMPLES to sneeze to hit
to leave to remain

Regular Verbs

(1) Regular verbs add *d* or *ed* to the infinitive to show the past tense.

EXAMPLES	INFINITIVE	PAST
	hope	hoped
	clean	cleaned
	move	moved

Irregular Verbs

(2) Irregular verbs may change form to show past tense, but they do not add *ed* or *d*.

EXAMPLES	INFINITIVE	PAST
	come	came
	have	had
	write	wrote
	sit	sat

EXERCISE 6 Number a sheet of paper 1–8. Write the past forms of the following verbs. Put *R* or *I* next to each verb to show whether it is regular or irregular. You may look these up in a dictionary.

EXAMPLE weave

1. arrive
2. eat
3. help
4. throw
5. run
6. gasp
7. swing
8. go

ADVERBS

2c An adverb is a word used to modify an action verb, an adjective, or another adverb.

Adverbs that modify action verbs tell *when, where, how, how much,* or *how often* action occurs.

An adverb can tell *when* something happens.

EXAMPLES Karen worked *late.*
[When did Karen work? Answer: *late.*]

Tomorrow Ben will climb the ladder.
[When will Ben climb? Answer: *tomorrow.*]

EXERCISE 7 Copy the following sentences on a sheet of paper. In each sentence underline the adverb that tells when something happens. Draw an arrow from the adverb to the action verb it modifies.

EXAMPLE Chari Barnway flew home today.

Chari Barnway flew home today.

1. The sun shone yesterday.
2. It rained afterward.
3. The rain soaked the ground today.
4. Mrs. Kroak, the frog farmer, said the rain came late.
5. "On Sunday," she said, "it rains early."

An adverb can tell *where* something happened.

EXAMPLES We take complaints *here*.
[Where do we take complaints?
Answer: *here*.]

Leave the dog *outside*.
[Where should the dog be left?
Answer: *outside*.]

EXERCISE 8 Copy the following sentences on a sheet of paper. In each sentence underline the adverb that tells where something happened. Draw an arrow from the adverb to the verb it modifies.

EXAMPLE The new students eat there.

The new students eat there.

1. Please step inside.
2. The bats sleep upstairs.
3. The crocodile crawls downstairs.
4. You will find trouble everywhere.
5. Perhaps we should talk outside.

An adverb can tell *how, how much,* or *how often* something happened.

EXAMPLES Maude Burger rested *calmly*.
[How did Maude rest? Answer: *calmly*.]

Irene Hogg cried *nightly*.
[How often did Irene cry? Answer: *nightly*.]

EXERCISE 9 Copy the following sentences on a sheet of paper. Draw a line under each adverb that tells how or how often. Draw an arrow from the adverb to the verb it modifies.

EXAMPLE Sally Spider moves slowly.

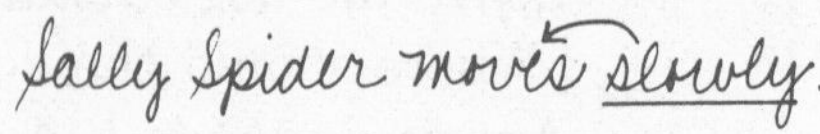

1. Sally spins her web carefully.
2. She weaves the sticky strands steadily.
3. She works instinctively.
4. Flies and moths struggle helplessly.
5. Sally stings them quickly.
6. She eats them slowly.
7. She waits patiently for more food.
8. She looks longingly at all flying insects.

EXERCISE 10 Number a sheet of paper 1–8. Each of the following sentences contains an adverb that tells where, when, or how something happens. After each number, write the adverb from the sentence. Next to each adverb, write *where, when,* or *how* to show what the adverb tells about the action.

EXAMPLE Pioneers moved westward.

westward, where

1. The government opened land gradually to settlers.
2. Some settlers farmed the land easily.
3. Most of them came hurriedly.
4. They started work early each day.
5. They farmed late into the night.
6. By the twentieth century, settlers were everywhere.

7. They worked unselfishly to produce large crops.
8. America harvests more grain yearly than any other country.

Adverbs sometimes modify adjectives.

See Adjective, p. 311

EXAMPLES Sheila is an *unusually* fast skater. [The adverb *unusually* modifies the adjective *fast,* which modifies the noun *skater.*]

She has a *really* busy schedule. [The adverb *really* modifies the adjective *busy,* which modifies the noun *schedule.*]

EXERCISE 11 Copy the following sentences on a sheet of paper. Underline each adverb that modifies an adjective. Draw an arrow from the adverb to the adjective.

EXAMPLE Some magicians perform amazingly difficult tricks.

Some magicians perform

amazingly difficult tricks.

1. Zenia Quickhand does surprisingly simple tricks.
2. She executes them in an astonishingly quick way.
3. Her hands are unbelievably fast.
4. Some of her tricks seem absolutely impossible.
5. The one with the vanishing egg is especially interesting.

Adverbs sometimes modify other adverbs.

EXAMPLES This winter the first snow fell *unusually* early.
[The adverb *unusually* modifies the adverb *early,* which modifies the verb *fell.*]

The moose called *quite* clearly.
[*Quite* modifies the adverb *clearly,* which modifies the verb *called.*]

EXERCISE 12 Copy the following sentences on a sheet of paper. Underline the adverb that modifies another adverb in each sentence. Draw an arrow from the first adverb to the adverb it modifies.

EXAMPLE Jim ducked very quickly.

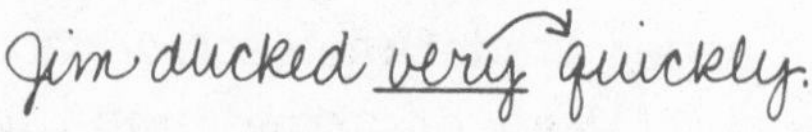
Jim ducked very quickly.

1. Jennie Ortega arrived unusually late.
2. She spoke quite hurriedly.
3. Her hands fluttered terribly fast.
4. Her eyes moved unusually rapidly.
5. She stopped talking quite suddenly.
6. She remained almost completely silent.
7. She had changed very quickly.
8. She left very early.

Hint: Many adverbs can be moved within a sentence.

EXAMPLES Jim *quickly* closed the box.
Quickly Jim closed the box.
Jim closed the box *quickly.*

2d Adverbs help compare actions of verbs.

Most short adverbs add **er** and **est** to show comparison. When only two actions are compared, use **er.** When three or more actions are compared, use **est.**

EXAMPLES Pattie Banner types *fast.*
Jim Post types *faster.*
Lillie Cranwell types *fastest* of all.

EXERCISE 13 Number a sheet of paper 1–5. After each number write the correct form of the adverb that belongs in the blank.

EXAMPLE European women seem to run ______ than American women. (fast)

faster

1. Possibly they train ______ than the Americans. (hard)
2. The East German women swimmers train ______ of all. (hard)
3. Some of them swim ______ than men. (fast)
4. East German gymnasts move ______ than Americans. (quick)
5. They leap the ______ of any athletes we have seen. (high)

Adverbs that end in **ly** do not add **er** or **est** to show comparison. These adverbs take the words *more* and *most* to show comparison.

EXAMPLES gracefully, more gracefully, most gracefully
shyly, more shyly, most shyly

EXERCISE 14 Number a sheet of paper 1–6. Write the correct form of the adverb that belongs in each blank.

EXAMPLE The lion cub snarled ______ than it had before. (angrily)

more angrily

1. The weather forecaster predicted sunny skies ______ than he had before. (boldly)
2. The clouds gathered ______ than we had ever seen them. (rapidly)
3. The gray clouds gathered ______ of all. (quickly)
4. Cars and buses moved ______ than usual. (cautiously)
5. In the future, the weather forecaster will make his predictions ______ than he had. (carefully)
6. We hope then he will predict the weather ______ of all. (accurately)

Irregular Adverbs

The adverbs *well* and *badly* change their forms in special ways to show comparison.

EXAMPLES Most birds swim *badly.*

Most birds swim *worse* than fish.

The weakest birds swim *worst* of all.

Most fish swim *well.*

Most fish swim *better* than birds.

Strong fish swim *best* of all.

EXERCISE 15 Number a sheet of paper 1–6. Write the correct form of the adverb that belongs in each blank.

EXAMPLE Monkeys climb trees ______ than humans. (well)

better

1. On tests of intelligence, monkeys do ______ than dogs. (well)
2. We have found that birds do ______ than dogs. (badly)
3. Birds do the ______ of all three. (badly)
4. Monkeys do the ______ of all three. (well)
5. Each animal can do something special ______ than the others. (well)
6. Even the smartest monkey cannot build a bird's nest ______ than a bird can. (well)

The words *not* and *never* are two special adverbs that do not change form. They make a verb, adjective, or adverb opposite in meaning.

EXAMPLES She *never* saw the car.
Vivian is *not* well.

PREPOSITIONS

See Noun, p. 325, Pronoun, p. 329

2e A preposition is a word used to relate a following noun or pronoun to some other words in a sentence.

EXAMPLES Joan left *before* noon.
[The preposition *before* relates *noon* to *left.*]

The money was hidden *in* the book.
[The preposition *in* relates *book* to *was hidden.*]

Seth cleared the bar *with* one leap.
[The preposition *with* relates *leap* to *cleared.*]

Prepositions often help show relationships of time, place, or manner.

EXAMPLES
TIME She left *after* the party.
PLACE She went *into* the cab.
MANNER She left *in* a hurry.

Here are some commonly used prepositions.

TIME		PLACE		MANNER
after	about	beside	up	by
before	above	down	among	except
during	across	into	to	for
since	against	near	on	like
until	around	over	near	of
	at	toward	along	with
	behind	under		
	below	through		

EXERCISE 16 Number a sheet of paper 1–10. After each number, write the preposition in each sentence.

EXAMPLE A skateboard rides like a surfboard.

like

1. Hawaiians found it was fun riding waves on a surfboard.
2. Not everyone lives near the ocean.
3. People who skim along the pavement need a board.
4. The first skateboard was a board tied to a roll-erskate.
5. Skateboards have changed since that day.
6. Today, professionally made skateboards whiz down hills.
7. Skateboard parks have opened throughout the country.
8. Skateboarders even have special language they use among themselves.
9. Bumps and bruises on knees and elbows are called "strawberries" and "hamburgers."
10. One day skateboarders may compete at the Olympics.

Object of the Preposition

The *object* of the preposition is the noun or pronoun that follows it. The preposition relates its object to some other word in the sentence. Usually that other word comes before the preposition.

In each of the following sentences, the preposition is underlined. The arrow points to its object.

EXAMPLES Andy came *at* midnight.

He stayed *in* the shadows.

A preposition may have more than one object.

EXAMPLES Andy naps *before* lunch and dinner.

He sleeps *on* the bed or the sofa.

EXERCISE 17 Copy each of the following sentences on a sheet of paper. Underline each preposition and draw an arrow from it to its object.

EXAMPLE Raise the flag up the pole.

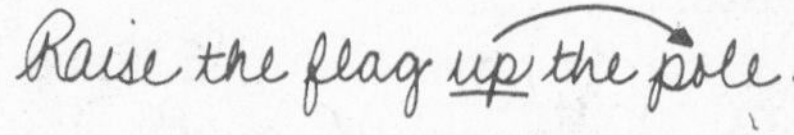
Raise the flag up the pole.

1. America's Civil War was fought in the United States.
2. The Union and the Confederacy drafted all able-bodied men into their ranks.
3. Large armies marched across the land.
4. Thousands fought upon the battlefields.
5. Many gave their lives for their ideals.
6. The two opposing generals, Grant and Lee, met at Appomatox.
7. This marked the end of the war.
8. Soldiers everywhere could return to their homes.
9. Peace settled across the land.
10. That was the last war within the United States.

CONJUNCTIONS

2f A conjunction is a word used to connect other words or groups of words.

Some common conjunctions are *and, but, for, nor,* and *or.* These conjunctions join words or word groups that are equal in meaning and form. They are called *coordinating conjunctions.*

Here is an example of a coordinating conjunction connecting words:

> Alex *and* Zenon are friends.
> [The conjunction *and* joins the names of two people who are friends.]

Here is an example of a coordinating conjunction connecting short word groups:

> Aletha raced down the stairs *and* across the hall.
> [The conjunction *and* joins the word groups *down the stairs* and *across the hall.*]

Here is an example of a coordinating conjunction connecting longer word groups:

> Alex saw Aletha, *but* she missed them completely.
> [The conjunction *but* joins the two complete thoughts *Alex saw Aletha* and *she missed them completely.*]

EXERCISE 18 Number a sheet of paper 1–6. Each of the following sentences needs a coordinating conjunction to complete it. After each number, write the coordinating conjunction needed in the blank in the sentence.

EXAMPLE "Kids are crazy ______ lovable," said Aletha's father.

but

1. Either Aletha races out, ______ she stays in her room.
2. She has many girl friends ______ a few boy friends.
3. They all like her, ______ no one really understands her.
4. She has tried to change for years, ______ I guess she will always be the same.
5. Neither her mother ______ I can figure out why she is like this.
6. We tell her we do not understand her, ______ she knows we love her very much.

Other conjunctions join word groups that are not equal in meaning or form. They are called *subordinating conjunctions.* Some of the common subordinating conjunctions are as follows.

after	unless
because	until
if	when
though	while

EXAMPLES We began to broadcast *after* we reached the moon.
We planned to explore its surface *if* we could walk.

EXERCISE 19 Number a sheet of paper 1–12. Each of the following sentences contains a coordinating or a subordinating conjunction. After each number write the coordinating or the subordinating conjunction in the sentence. Put *C* after every coordinating conjunction. If it is a subordinating conjunction, put *S* after it.

EXAMPLE They looked back after they had reached the peak.

1. They looked everywhere, but they saw no life.
2. They had hoped to find some when they had landed.
3. They were disappointed because their search seemed fruitless.
4. One of the explorers walked over the hill and disappeared from the others.
5. They noticed he was gone after they had called him on the intercom radio.
6. His disappearance frightened some of the explorers, but one woman remained calm.
7. "He may die unless we find him," she radioed.
8. The others gathered around her when she said this.
9. They made plans to find the lost explorer, for they hoped to save him.
10. While they were making their plans, the lost explorer walked back over the hill.
11. He was covered with dust but had suffered no harm.
12. He had heard them call on the radio, but his transmitter was not working.

INTERJECTIONS

2g An interjection is a word or word group used to express strong feeling.

EXAMPLES *Hurrah!* I won the prize.
Whoops! I didn't mean that.
We lost track of him, *curse the luck!*

An exclamation mark (!) often comes after an interjection or the sentence that contains it. An interjection in the middle of a sentence may be set off by commas.

EXAMPLE That horse, *alas,* belonged to my dear father.

EXERCISE 20 Number a sheet of paper 1–4. Next to each number, write the interjection you find in the sentence.

EXAMPLE Humph, I find it hard to believe that!
Humph

1. They have no right to do that, blast their hides!
2. Well, I can wait without your company.
3. If I possibly can, so help me Hannah, I'll fix you!
4. Her first reaction was, oh, what have we done this time!

WORDS AS DIFFERENT PARTS OF SPEECH

2h Some words can be used as different parts of speech.

Sometimes a word that acts as one part of speech in one sentence may act as a different part of speech in another sentence.

EXAMPLE The *airplane* swooped low.
Jane liked the *airplane* ride.
[In the first sentence, *airplane* acts as a noun; in the second sentence *airplane* is an adjective that helps describe what kind of a ride Jane had.]

REVIEW EXERCISE A **Complete Verb**

Number a sheet of paper 1–10. Next to each number write the complete verb (the main verb plus any helping verbs).

EXAMPLE Thomas Jefferson had hoped for peace with the British.

1. The leaders of the colonies asked for help from Jefferson.
2. He had practiced law in Virginia.
3. He knew the problems of the colonies.
4. He also could write well.
5. His friends suggested a special assignment for him.
6. The colonies needed a statement of their independence.
7. Jefferson left his wife and family in Virginia.
8. He spent most of the summer in Philadelphia.
9. There he wrote the Declaration of Independence.
10. Its words have been important for more than two hundred years.

REVIEW EXERCISE B **Action or Linking Verbs**

Number a sheet of paper 1–10. The verb in each of the following ten sentences is underlined. On your paper, tell whether each verb is an action verb or a linking verb.

EXAMPLE The English settlers sailed to America.

action

1. To the first settlers there, Jamestown looked like a place for finding gold.
2. One hundred twenty men settled in Jamestown in 1607.
3. Only twelve of these men were skilled workers.
4. Most of the men called themselves "gentlemen."
5. A gentleman never had done a day's work in his life.
6. John Smith ordered the men to dig wells and to build shelters.
7. Smith traveled to Indian settlements for corn and meat.
8. John Smith was a harsh ruler.
9. His rules seemed strict.
10. Every morning the men marched to their jobs to the beat of a drum.

REVIEW EXERCISE C **Identifying Verbs**

Copy each of the following sentences on a sheet of paper. Underline the verb in each sentence.

EXAMPLE Early settlers in Jamestown ate corn.

Carly settlers in Jamestown ate corn.

1. Some of the men at Jamestown cut wood.
2. They hated hard physical work.
3. They feared starvation, especially in the winter of 1610.
4. At this time ships from England brought fresh supplies.
5. In 1609, King James gave more land to the Virginia colony.
6. Native Americans also helped the colonists.
7. These original Americans grew tobacco.
8. Within a few years, American colonists were shipping tobacco to England.
9. King James considered smoking harmful to the brain.
10. The English still wanted tobacco.

REVIEW EXERCISE D Adverbs

An adverb is underlined in each of the following sentences. Number a sheet of paper 1–10. Copy the adverb in each sentence. Then list the verb, adjective, or adverb that it modifies.

EXAMPLE Being late can be quite embarrassing.

quite, embarrassing

1. Felicita knew well that she would be late.
2. She quickly grabbed her books and ran.
3. Suddenly she stopped running.
4. She was unusually late, but she had to have her lunch money.
5. She ran home faster than she had ever run before.
6. Her heart beat uncomfortably when she could not find her house key.
7. The door opened easily and Felicita ran to the kitchen.
8. She often left her lunch money on the kitchen table.
9. She found the money there.
10. By lunch time Felicita was tired, but she was not very hungry.

REVIEW EXERCISE E Prepositions

Copy each of the following sentences on a sheet of paper. Fill in each blank with a preposition. You may want to look at the list of prepositions on page 44.

EXAMPLE Our school played its first baseball game ______ April 1.

Our school played its first baseball game on April 1.

1. The baseball game was played ______ the school yard.
2. The only good ball rolled ______ the school fence.

3. Then a bat broke and the star batter threw the pieces ______ the pitcher.
4. Everyone ______ the coach was angry.
5. It started to rain ______ the game.
6. As the team moved ______ the field, one member slipped.
7. She had to be carried ______ the field.
8. A doctor arrived and put a splint ______ her leg.
9. Because she lived ______ the school, the injured player was carried home.
10. When she was settled ______ her home, she asked who had won that terrible game.

REVIEW EXERCISE F Verbs, Adverbs, Prepositions, Conjunctions

Number a sheet of paper 1–25. Write each of the numbered word or words. Identify the word or words as *verb, adverb, preposition,* or *conjunction.*

EXAMPLE

The value [1]*of* what Native Americans [2]*have given* the world [3]*is* [4]*very* great. People throughout the world will be [5]*forever* [6]*in* their debt, [7]*because* many of the foods grown [8]*and* eaten [9]*today* [10]*come* from plants discovered and first grown [11]*by* the first Americans.

The shelves [12]*of* our stores are filled [13]*with* these foods. Our eating habits [14]*would be* [15]*quite* different [16]*if* we did not have corn, tomatoes, white [17]*and* sweet potatoes, and many kinds [18]*of* beans. Could we eat [19]*well* [20]*without* peanuts, chestnuts, pumpkins, strawberries, blackberries, [21]*or* cranberries? We [22]*would miss* maple syrup. How [23]*could* we [23]*have* a real Thanksgiving dinner [24]*with* no turkey? We [25]*should thank* Native Americans for all of these foods.

CHAPTER

3

PHRASES

Verb Phrases, Prepositional Phrases, Noun Phrases

The first two chapters in this textbook describe how single words act as parts of speech. This chapter deals with groups of words that act together as parts of speech. The groups of words that are used in this way are called *phrases.*

KINDS OF PHRASES

3a A phrase is a group of related words used as a single part of speech.

A phrase is a group of words that are closely related. For example, consider this sentence.

The girl in the window is my friend.

The phrase *in the window* acts as an adjective that modifies the noun *girl.* The phrase tells which girl is the friend. In the sentence *She should have been thinner,* the phrase *should have been* acts as a linking verb.

A phrase may act as a noun, an adjective, an adverb, or a verb. The three most common types of phrases are the *noun phrase,* the *verb phrase,* and the *prepositional phrase.*

Noun Phrases

See Noun, p. 325

3b A noun phrase contains a noun and its modifiers.

EXAMPLES *The old car* blocked *the busy highway.*
[The noun *car* has the modifiers *the* and *old.* These three words make up a noun phrase. The noun *highway* has the modifiers *the* and *busy.* These three words make up another noun phrase.]

Other cars had to make *a quick detour.*
[The noun *cars* and its modifier *other* make up a noun phrase. The noun *detour* and its modifiers *a* and *quick* make up another noun phrase.]

A noun phrase can be replaced with a pronoun.

EXAMPLES *The old car* blocked the busy highway.
It blocked the busy highway.

Other cars had to make a quick detour.
They had to make a quick detour.

EXERCISE 1 Copy the following sentences on a sheet of paper. Underline each noun phrase. Be sure to underline the modifiers that go with the noun.

EXAMPLE The new movie has several young actors.

The new movie has several young actors.

1. The new actors are talented children.
2. The young actors play rugged settlers.
3. Yellow yapping dogs play their animal friends.
4. This American film was made in England.
5. It has stormed the western world.
6. It has already made a large profit.

Verb Phrases

3c A verb phrase is made up of the main verb and its helpers.

See Verbs, pp. 29–35

The main verb in a sentence may describe an action. Or the verb may begin a description of someone or something.

EXAMPLE The movie *played* for two weeks.
It *was* popular.

Sometimes the main verb has one or more helping verbs.

EXAMPLES The movie *had played* for two weeks.
The movie *had been playing* for two weeks.

The main verb and its helpers make up a *verb phrase.* This kind of phrase may also be called the *complete verb.*

Hint: Remember that the verb phrase must include both a main verb and its helping verbs.

EXERCISE 2 Copy each of the following sentences on a sheet of paper. Underline the verb phrase in each sentence. Remember to underline both the main verb and the helping verbs.

EXAMPLE John Cassisi had been a student in a junior high in Brooklyn.
John Cassisi had been a student in a junior high in Brooklyn.

1. One day a strange man had come into John's class.
2. The man was looking for young actors.
3. He had seen John at a desk.
4. John had been working on his lessons.
5. He had noticed the stranger.
6. The man had spoken a few words to John.
7. "We will want you for a movie."
8. John had said nothing.

9. He had listened carefully, though.
10. He had been given a part in a new movie.

Prepositional Phrases

3d A prepositional phrase begins with a preposition and usually ends with a noun or a pronoun.

See Prepositions, p. 329

EXAMPLES *in the movie*
at the beginning
on the table
before the end

The noun or pronoun in the prepositional phrase is called the *object* of the preposition. Words that modify the object of the preposition are also part of the prepositional phrase.

EXAMPLE He showed the movie *in a dusty, empty barn.*
[In this example, *in* is the preposition. *Barn* is its object. The other words *a, dusty,* and *empty* are modifiers. Together the words make a prepositional phrase.]

Hint: Do not confuse a prepositional phrase beginning with *to* with the infinitive form of a verb, for example, *to go.* Remember that a prepositional phrase always has an object.

See Infinitive, p. 323

EXERCISE 3 Number a sheet of paper 1–10. Write the complete prepositional phrase in each sentence. Underline the preposition and draw an arrow to its object in the prepositional phrase.

EXAMPLE We live on the fourth floor.

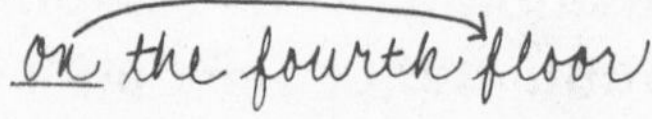

1. Once we lived near the front door.
2. Then we moved to the fourth floor.
3. The upper floors have a fire escape at the back.
4. The fire escape leads to an alley.
5. There is a large waste bin under the window.
6. The trash men come early and collect trash from the bin.
7. I can watch them from our back window.
8. They come on Saturday.
9. They make too much noise in the alley.
10. My dad wishes they would come late in the day.

See Adjective, p. 311

(1) A prepositional phrase may be used as an adjective.

A prepositional phrase that is used as an adjective modifies a noun or pronoun. The noun or pronoun that the phrase modifies is not part of the prepositional phrase. The noun or pronoun usually comes just before the phrase.

EXAMPLES The dress *in the window* is expensive.
[The phrase *in the window* tells which dress is expensive. The phrase is used as an adjective to modify the noun *dress.*]

You *in the front row seats* should move back.
[The phrase *in the front row seats* modifies the pronoun *you*. The phrase is used as an adjective modifying the pronoun *you*.]

A prepositional phrase used as an adjective helps to answer the questions *what kind? which one?* or *how many?*

EXERCISE 4 Number a sheet of paper 1–10. The following sentences contain prepositional phrases used as adjectives. Next to each number write the prepositional phrase. Next to the phrase, write the word it modifies.

EXAMPLE Watching birds gave people a good idea for a glider.

for a glider, idea

1. More than a hundred years ago one of the bird watchers was Otto Lilienthal.
2. He decided to build a glider with large wings.
3. Many people around the world had tried building large gliders.
4. None of the gliders could carry a person safely.
5. Lilienthal had a better idea for his glider.
6. He built light wings of canvas.
7. He grabbed a point near the middle and ran downhill fast.
8. He accomplished a flight of fifteen seconds.
9. Later he made many flights of longer times.
10. His early success with a glider made aviation history.

See Adverb, p. 311

(2) A prepositional phrase may be used as an adverb.

Most prepositional phrases that are used as adverbs modify a verb.

EXAMPLES The geese came *at daybreak.* [The prepositional phrase tells *when* the geese came.]

They landed *at the lake's edge.* [The prepositional phrase tells *where* they landed.]

They beat the air *with their wings.* [This prepositional phrase tells *how* they beat the air.]

They stayed *throughout the day.* [This prepositional phrase tells *how long* they stayed.]

Sometimes a prepositional phrase used as an adverb modifies an adjective. Other times it modifies an adverb.

EXAMPLES Their wings seem too large *for their bodies.* [The prepositional phrase modifies the adjective *large.*]

They left late *in the afternoon.* [The prepositional phrase modifies the adverb *late.*]

Hint: A prepositional phrase that is used as an adverb helps to answer these questions: *when? where? how? how long?* or *how much?*

EXERCISE 5 Number a sheet of paper 1–10. The following sentences contain prepositional phrases used as adverbs. Next to each number, write the prepositional phrase. Next to the phrase write the word it modifies.

EXAMPLE Gliders fly best in a wind.

in a wind, fly

1. Octave Chanute lived near Chicago, where he built the first successful American glider.
2. Ten years later the Wright brothers experimented with gliders.
3. They soared at Kitty Hawk, North Carolina.
4. The sea breezes kept them above the beach.
5. Orville Wright stayed airborne for ten minutes.
6. Later a Californian lifted his glider with a balloon.
7. The balloon raised him and his glider above two thousand feet.
8. Then he glided safely to earth.
9. Fifty years ago Frank Hawks flew his glider across the United States.
10. An airplane towed him for thirty-six hours and forty-seven minutes.

REVIEW EXERCISE A Noun Phrases

Copy the following sentences on a sheet of paper. Fill in each blank with a noun phrase. Use the list of suggestions that follows the sentences.

EXAMPLE Many Americans eat ______.

Many Americans eat fresh eggs.

1. ______ eats many times during the day.
2. He may eat ______ for breakfast.
3. During the morning he may have time for ______.
4. His lunch will include a ham sandwich, fruit, and ______.
5. ______ makes the best after-school snack.

a hungry boy	fresh eggs
a fat man	hot cereal
a puppy	crunchy granola
the growing boy	a quick snack
a parakeet	other foods
a hot day	a fresh peach

REVIEW EXERCISE B Verb Phrases

You will find thirteen verb phrases (complete verbs) in the following paragraphs. Number a sheet of paper 1–13 and write each of the verb phrases. Notice that *not* is an adverb; it is not part of the complete verb.

EXAMPLE

In 1791 Boston experienced a terrible epidemic of smallpox. Before the epidemic had ended, more than half of the citizens had been stricken. More than 800 people had died. Doctors could not control the disease.

Then Cotton Mather was told about a method of controlling smallpox. He first heard of this method from an African slave. The method was known as inoculation. Serum from an infected person was injected into the skin of a healthy person. The healthy person might become sick, but he or she would not die. After recovering, this person would be forever immune to smallpox.

Many doctors had long feared inoculation. Cotton Mather was even called a murderer. However, inoculation is now widely used to prevent smallpox.

REVIEW EXERCISE C Prepositional Phrases

Number a sheet of paper 1–10. Then list the prepositional phrase in each sentence. Next draw an arrow from the preposition to the object of the preposition.

EXAMPLE Hermits often live in a small hut.

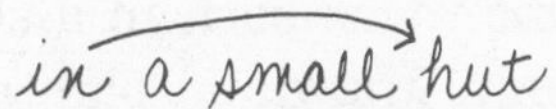

1. The treasure hunt began in an empty lot.
2. Hunters looked under the bushes.

3. The first clue was hidden beneath a tree.
4. It told the treasure hunters to walk four paces past the firehouse.
5. They found the next clue on a fire hydrant.
6. They walked along a picket fence.
7. When they reached a white house with green trim, they found the last clue.
8. It sent them down a long, winding hill.
9. At the bottom they found the treasure.
10. By then they were too tired to care that it was a watermelon.

REVIEW EXERCISE D Prepositional Phrases

A prepositional phrase is underlined in each sentence below. Write each sentence on a sheet of paper. Draw an arrow from the prepositional phrase to the word that it modifies. Then write *adv.* or *adj.* to tell whether the phrase acts as an adverb or an adjective.

EXAMPLE Harriet Tubman was a very old woman when she died in 1913.

Harriet Tubman was a very old woman when she died in 1913., adv.

1. Harriet Tubman was born in a slave cabin.
2. As a slave on a Maryland plantation, she was not allowed to learn to read or write.
3. On a dark night she ran way from the plantation.
4. She was guided only by the North Star.

5. As a free woman, she returned to slave territory to resuce other slaves.
6. Slave owners once offered a reward of $40,000 for her capture.
7. The main idea of her life was to free people from slavery.
8. During the Civil War, Harriet Tubman worked as a scout, a spy, and a cook.
9. She also organized small bands of nurses.
10. After the war she lived in Auburn, New York.
11. She provided a home for her parents whom she had rescued from slavery.
12. The story of Harriet Tubman is told in a book called *Harriet Tubman: The Moses of Her People*.
13. The book was written by Harriet Tubman's friend, Sarah Bradford.
14. Harriet Tubman's story remains an inspiration to all freedom-loving people.
15. She gained greatness through service.

CHAPTER

4

SENTENCES

Sentences, Clauses, Sentence Problems

People use more than just single words to communicate. They combine words in ways to make their meanings clear. The basic combinations of words that make meanings clear are called *sentences*.

Sentences are formed in different ways. It is important to study these ways so that you can write clear, useful sentences.

SENTENCES

4a A sentence is a group of related words that makes a complete thought.

A sentence begins with a capital letter and ends with a period, a question mark, or an exclamation mark.

These examples are sentences.

Bands played.
Clowns juggled.
The circus, with all its action, noise, color, and smell, had arrived.
Have you been to the circus?
You can hardly believe your eyes!

These examples are not sentences.

Colorful bands
Juggled and danced
The circus with all its action, noise, color, and smell
to the circus
can hardly believe

EXERCISE 1 Number a sheet of paper 1–8. Some of the following word groups are sentences. Some are not. Write *S* next to each number of a sentence. Write *N* next to each number of a group of words that are not a sentence.

EXAMPLE Covering an entire floor

N

1. Whispers in the pine tree
2. The whispering wind
3. A building collapsed
4. Buses came and went
5. A pigeon on the ledge
6. The can rolled against the pole
7. A cave under the ground
8. Ghana became independent

4b A simple sentence must contain a subject and a predicate.

Every group of words that contains a complete thought must have two important parts: a *subject* and a *predicate.*

(1) The subject is what the sentence tells about.

The *complete subject* of a sentence is always a noun or a pronoun. It may be a group of words that serves as a noun or pronoun. The group may include words that help describe the noun or pronoun.

EXAMPLES *Judith* is an interesting girl. [The noun *Judith* tells who is described by the rest of the sentence.]

The first ten girls caught colds. [The noun *girls* and the adjectives *the, first,* and *ten* tell who caught colds.]

If the subject is removed, the words no longer make a sentence.

EXAMPLES is an interesting girl
caught colds

The one noun or pronoun that is part of the complete subject is called the *simple subject.*

EXAMPLES *Judith* is an interesting girl. [The noun *Judith* is the simple subject.]

The first ten *girls* caught colds. [The noun *girls* is the simple subject.]

Sometimes a single word alone may be the subject of a sentence. In that case it is both the simple subject and the complete subject.

EXAMPLES *Judith* is an interesting girl.
They ran all the way.
Susan called my name.

Hint: Remember that prepositional phrases are modifiers, not subjects. No part of a prepositional phrase may be a simple subject of a sentence.

EXAMPLE The eerie-sounding wind *in the trees* kept me awake.
[*Wind* is the simple subject.]

EXERCISE 2 Number a sheet of paper 1–10. Write out the complete subject of each sentence. Circle the simple subject.

EXAMPLE The prancing white horse tossed its head.
The prancing white horse

1. The first automobiles were like carriages without horses.
2. These machines were far less powerful than cars today.
3. Paved roads were built all across the country.
4. The noisy rattles of old cars finally disappeared.
5. Automobile factories grew in cities in the Northern states.

6. Soon the noise of trucks and cars filled the cities.
7. Airplanes carried travelers through the skies.
8. Tractors replaced the horses and mules on the farms.
9. Scientists invented rockets and satellites.
10. A plane zoomed across the sky faster than the speed of sound!

(2) The predicate tells something about the subject.

The *complete predicate* is always a verb and the related words that tell about the subject of the sentence.

EXAMPLES John *ate quickly.*
[The verb *ate* and the adverb *quickly* tell what John did.]

His sister *has written in the book.*
[The verb *has written* and the prepositional phrase *in the book* together tell what his sister did.]

If the predicate is removed, the words no longer make a sentence.

EXAMPLES John
His sister

See Verb, p. 332

Every complete predicate must contain a verb. The complete verb that is made up of the main verb and any helping verbs is called the *simple predicate.*

EXAMPLES John *ate quickly.*
[The verb *ate* is the simple predicate.]

His sister *has written* in the book. [The main verb *written* and the helping verb *has* together are the simple predicate.]

Hint: A sentence cannot have a subject without a predicate or a predicate without a subject.

EXERCISE 3 Number a sheet of paper 1–10. Write out the complete predicate of each sentence. Put a box around the simple predicate.

EXAMPLE They roamed the earth.

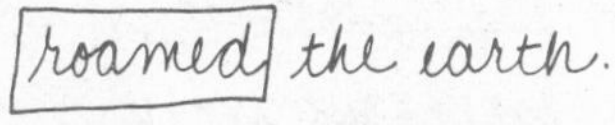

1. Dinosaurs ruled the earth millions of years ago.
2. The word *dinosaur* comes from the Greek words for "terrible lizard."
3. These animals grew to many sizes.
4. They lived in Europe, Asia, Africa, and North America.
5. Some of them ate meat.
6. Others were considered plant eaters.
7. Their brains were very small.
8. Some museums display the bones of dinosaurs.
9. One skeleton is twenty feet tall and forty feet long.
10. Such a beast gives meaning to the word *dinosaur.*

Compound Subject and Compound Predicate

(3) A sentence with more than one subject has a compound subject.

Compound subjects are usually joined by the conjunctions *and, or,* or *but.*

EXAMPLE *All of the pups* but *only two of the kittens* were missing.

EXERCISE 4 Copy the following six sentences on a sheet of paper. Underline both parts of the compound subject. Circle the simple subjects.

EXAMPLES Several women but only two men were there.

Several women but only two men were there.

The lion and the tiger snarled at the trainer.

The lion and the tiger snarled at the trainer.

1. Wolves and foxes are quite scarce.
2. Many ranchers and farmers dislike wolves.
3. Foxes and wolves kill warm-blooded animals for food.
4. A male wolf and a female wolf stay together.
5. Aunts and uncles help care for the pups.
6. Rabbits and deer alike flee from the yelping youngsters.

(4) A sentence with more than one verb has a compound predicate.

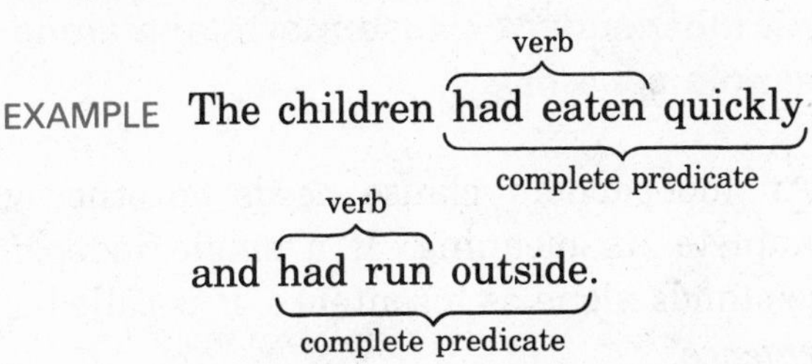

verb
EXAMPLE The children had eaten quickly
complete predicate
verb
and had run outside.
complete predicate

EXERCISE 5 Number a sheet of paper 1–5. Each of the following sentences has a compound predicate. After each number write both parts of the compound predicate.

EXAMPLE Randy Chavez walked up Center Street and stopped at the mailbox.

walked up Center Street,
stopped at the mailbox

1. He reached carefully in his pocket and took out a square, grey envelope.
2. He opened the envelope and removed a piece of red paper.
3. He licked the flap and then sealed the envelope.
4. He pulled down the mailbox door and dropped in the envelope.
5. He stuffed the valentine into his pocket and turned for home.

Clauses

4c A clause is a group of related words containing a subject and a predicate.

A clause may be *independent* or *dependent.*

(1) An independent clause may stand alone as a simple sentence.

An independent clause needs no other words to complete its meaning. If a single independent clause stands alone as a sentence, it is called a *simple sentence.*

EXAMPLES She is trying.
[*She* is the subject; *is trying* is the predicate.]

You could do that.
[*You* is the subject; *could do that* is the predicate.]

(2) A dependent clause cannot stand alone.

A dependent clause must be a part of a sentence. It needs an independent clause to complete its meaning.

EXAMPLES because she won (dependent clause)
We applauded *because she won.*
[The independent clause *We applauded* is added to the dependent clause to make a sentence.]

after they ate (dependent clause)
They left *after they ate.*
[The independent clause *They left* is added to the dependent clause to make a sentence.]

Both independent clauses and dependent clauses have subjects and predicates. A dependent clause often begins with a subordinate conjunction, such as *because, when, since,* or *after.*

See Conjunction, p. 316

EXERCISE 6 Number a sheet of paper 1–10. Some of the following word groups are independent clauses. Some are dependent clauses. Identify each word group as an independent clause *I* or a dependent clause *D*.

EXAMPLES Before we ate dinner

She left before dinner

1. I understand your reasons
2. Until you tell others
3. Everyone will think the wrong thoughts
4. You must be frank
5. If you fail
6. When you speak
7. People often make mistakes
8. Because they remain silent
9. The mistakes only seem worse
10. Honesty requires openness as well as good thoughts

(3) A compound sentence is made up of two or more independent clauses.

A compound sentence may have any number of independent clauses. Most compound sentences are made up of two independent clauses joined by a comma and a coordinating conjunction, such as *or, and,* or *but.*

EXAMPLES Marsha set the table, *and* Tom cooked the dinner.
I like wrestling, *but* I dislike boxing.
Tana will build the set, *or* we won't have one!

If a compound sentence has three or more independent clauses, the coordinating conjunction comes before the final clause.

EXAMPLES I tried, I failed, *but* I didn't quit.
We ate breakfast, we cleaned up our dishes, *and* then we left.
Sometime before midnight the fire caught hold, the wolves stopped howling, the moon came out, *and* the sentry relaxed.

See Punctuation, pp. 228–230

A semicolon (;) may substitute in a compound sentence for both the comma and the coordinating conjunction. This kind of punctuation is best when the clauses are closely related.

EXAMPLES Don likes sandwiches on rye bread; I like mine on white bread.

Mom made Jack clean up the yard; she made me clean the house.

EXERCISE 7 Number a sheet of paper 1–10. Some of the following sentences are simple sentences.

Some are compound sentences. Label each sentence as simple *S* or compound *C*.

EXAMPLE After school, we played soccer.

1. School is not really so bad, but I could do without the homework.
2. I would rather be out playing basketball, or I might watch TV.
3. My brother is in high school, and he likes work.
4. Right after dinner, he disappears into his bedroom.
5. He reads until bedtime, but I get tired.
6. He learns new things from his books.
7. His only other interests are collecting sea shells or girl friends.
8. He even has a dried seahorse, but he keeps it locked up.
9. Reading keeps him from going to a baseball game.
10. He misses a lot of home runs and excitement.

(4) A complex sentence is made up of one or more dependent clauses added to an independent clause.

EXAMPLES I enjoy swimming *because it is good exercise.*

After the car stalled, we walked home.

That is the boy *who stopped the terrible fight.*

EXERCISE 8 Number a sheet of paper 1–6. Following are six sentences. Identify each as a simple sentence *S*, a compound sentence *C*, or a complex sentence *Cx*.

EXAMPLES The man in the middle of the whole thing would not say anything about the incident.

S

After Draper won, the other girls congratulated her.

Cx

1. When we were in California, we visited Los Angeles and San Francisco.
2. My sister, Elizabeth, had never seen the Pacific Ocean.
3. We crossed the Bay Bridge to Oakland; there we visited our relatives, the Tregaskys.
4. Because Mr. Tregasky is a football fan, he offered to take us to see the Raiders play.
5. On our way back to Indiana we stopped at Yosemite and watched the bears, but nothing else exciting happened after that.
6. Nothing happened on the return trip until Dad left his suitcase in a motel in Salt Lake City.

Purposes of Sentences

4d Sentences are used for four different purposes.

(1) A sentence may declare a fact, an opinion, or a feeling.

This kind of sentence is called a *declarative sentence.*

EXAMPLES The shadows darkened the valley.
That doesn't taste very good.
I dislike insects.

Declarative sentences usually end with a period.

(2) A sentence may ask a question.

This kind of sentence is called an *interrogative sentence.*

EXAMPLES Did the police interrogate the robber?
Who drew this picture?
What time is it?

Many interrogative sentences switch the normal declarative order of the simple subject and verb.

EXAMPLES It is noon.
Is it noon?

You were at home.
Were you at home?

Some interrogative sentences use a form of *do* as a beginning helping verb.

EXAMPLES The trains run on time.
Do the trains run on time?

The robber confessed.
Did the robber confess?

Interrogative sentences end with a question mark.

(3) A sentence may request or order something.

This kind of sentence is called an *imperative sentence.*

EXAMPLES Please close the door.
Meet me at the theater at noon.
Show me where you found it.

Imperative sentences usually omit the subject *you*. When the subject is omitted, it is said to be "understood." Imperative sentences end with a period.

(4) A sentence may express shock or surprise.

This kind of sentence is called an *exclamatory sentence.*

EXAMPLES "I don't believe it!" she exclaimed.
"That does it—I quit!"

An exclamatory sentence often ends with an exclamation mark.

EXERCISE 9 End punctuation has been omitted from the following sentences. Copy each sentence and add the end punctuation. Then identify each sentence as declarative *D,* interrogative *I,* imperative *Im,* or exclamatory *E.*

EXAMPLE Can you darn socks

1. You meant to catch me, you rat
2. What did you have in mind

3. Stop doing that
4. I can see you have no plans
5. Make plans immediately
6. What an astounding idea
7. I suppose I should go along with you
8. Where will it all end
9. Go directly into his office
10. We have a contract to make the world's best mousetrap

Completers

Every sentence must contain at least one verb. Often the complete predicate will contain another important word as well. This kind of word is called a *completer* because it completes or makes clear what the subject and verb are telling about. Completers may be either *objects* or *subject completers*.

See Verb, p. 332.

4e The direct object receives the action of the verb.

EXAMPLE Terry hit the ball.
[The ball received the action of the verb *hit*.]

Hint: Here are the steps to find the direct object of an action verb.

Find the verb. *(hit)*
Ask: *Who or what hit?*
Answer: *Terry*
Ask *Who or what did Terry hit?*
Answer: *ball*
Ball is the direct object.

EXERCISE 10 Number a sheet of paper 1–6. Write the direct object of the action verb in each sentence.

EXAMPLE Sally ate the meat.

meat

1. Bill De Souza opened his eyes wide.
2. Then he lifted his lunch box from the fence post.
3. He opened the lid.
4. Carefully, Bill picked out a jar of pickles.
5. From inside the jar he pulled out a green pickle.
6. He quickly popped the pickle into his mouth!

4f The subject completer follows the linking verb and completes the meaning of the sentence.

The subject completer may be a noun, a pronoun, an adjective, or an adverb.

EXAMPLES Sarah seems friendly.
[The adjective *friendly* completes the meaning of the sentence by telling how Sarah seems.]

Mr. Williams is my teacher.
[The noun *teacher* completes the meaning of the sentence by telling who Mr. Williams is.]

Hint: Here are the steps to follow to find the subject completer.

Find the linking verb. In the first example above, the verb is *seems*.
Find the subject. Ask "*Who or what seems?*"
The answer: *Sarah*.
Then ask, "*Sarah seems who or what?*"
The answer is *friendly*. *Friendly* is the subject completer.

EXERCISE 11 Following are five unfinished sentences. Copy each sentence and complete it by adding a noun, a pronoun, an adjective, or an adverb.

1. My father became ______.
2. He is usually ______.
3. The winner was ______.
4. He looked ______.
5. That may be ______ now.

Sentence Patterns

The English language has a few basic sentence patterns. Most of the thousands and thousands of sentences you and your English-speaking friends and neighbors speak fit one of these patterns. The most common of these patterns are given here.

Sentence Pattern 1 SUBJECT-VERB (S-V)

EXAMPLES The child (S) fell (V).
Then he (S) cried (V).

In Sentence Pattern 1, only the simple subject and the main verb make up the basic pattern. Modifiers do not change the pattern. Sometimes this pattern has an adverb following the verb.

EXAMPLES
S V Adv.
The man fell down.
S V Adv.
They went home.
S V Prep. phrase
They laughed about the joke.
[The prepositional phrase *about the joke* is used as an adverb.]

Occasionally the word *here* or *there* will be in the position of the subject. An example is *Here is the button.* This pattern is a variation of the S-V sentence pattern. The noun or pronoun following the verb is the true subject of the sentence. *Button* is the subject of the sentence *Here is the button.*

Sentence Pattern 2 **SUBJECT-VERB-DIRECT OBJECT (S-V-DO)**

EXAMPLES
S V DO
Our team scored a run.
S V DO
Then the other team got a run.
S V DO
Next Peggy hit a home run.
S V DO
We won the game.

A sentence in Pattern 2 may have words or phrases added to the basic pattern.

EXAMPLE
S V DO
Wanda gave a purse to Jody for Christmas.

A variation is possible in the pattern of this sentence. The phrase *to Jody* can be moved in front of the direct object *purse*. The preposition *to* disappears. The result is *Wanda gave Jody a purse for Christmas*. In this sentence, *Jody* is called the *indirect object*.

Sentence Pattern 2 has this variation:

Sentence Pattern 2a **SUBJECT-VERB-INDIRECT OBJECT-DIRECT OBJECT (S-V-IO-DO)**

EXAMPLES

S V IO DO
Dad loaned Jim the car.

Jim gave me a ride.

Jim showed me his driving.

Dad may buy Jim a car.

Note that Pattern 2a sentences may be rewritten as regular Pattern 2 sentences. To do this, a prepositional phrase is used instead of the indirect object. When a prepositional phrase is used, it follows the direct object.

EXAMPLES

S V IO DO
I made Janet a sweater.
[Pattern 2a]

S V DO Prep. phrase
I made a sweater for Janet.
[Pattern 2 with a prepositional phrase]

S V IO DO
She made Tom some iced tea.
[Pattern 2a]

S V DO Prep. phrase
She made some iced tea for Tom.
[Pattern 2 with a prepositional phrase.]

EXERCISE 12 Number a sheet of paper 1–10. Label each sentence as Pattern 1 (S-V), Pattern 2 (S-V-O), or Pattern 2a (S-V-IO-DO).

EXAMPLES The dog fell into the well behind the barn.

Pattern 1 (S-V)

I gave Anne a piece of my cake.

Pattern 2a (S-V-IO-DO)

1. Life in America has changed since the 1800's.
2. Wealthy people once built themselves large homes.
3. Several generations lived together.
4. Grandma and Mother ruled the household.
5. The family ate in a separate dining room.
6. Rich families usually hired a cook or a maid.
7. The maid served the family three meals a day.
8. Servants worked hard.
9. Few families hire full-time servants now.
10. In each generation, our style of life changes.

EXERCISE 13 Rewrite each Pattern 2a sentence as a Pattern 2 sentence.

EXAMPLE He told me the truth.

He told the truth to me.

1. Mark offered Millie a colorful scarf for her hair.
2. She flashed him a little smile.
3. He blurted, "I buy everybody presents this time of the year."
4. "You mean you didn't make me this?" she asked.
5. "No, but I rented Buddy my motorcycle for the money to buy it," he answered.
6. "Now you can't give me a ride so I can wear it," moaned Millie.

Sentence Pattern 3 SUBJECT-LINKING VERB-SUBJECT COMPLETER (S-LV-SC)

	S	LV	SC
EXAMPLES	She	is	president.
	Johnson	became	my rival.
	Ed	is	my friend.

All of the completers in these examples are nouns. The noun completer always renames the subject.

All of the completers in the following examples are adjectives.

Sandra seems *angry*.
Tony became quite *ill*.
That looks *great*.

All of the completers in the following examples are adverbs.

The answer is *there*.
Myrna is *downtown*.

EXERCISE 14 Number a sheet of paper 1–8. Write out each completer in the following sentences. Label each as a noun or an adjective.

EXAMPLE Ferdinand was a king.
king, noun

1. My grandpa was a carpenter.
2. His home was a huge house.
3. Today big old houses are unpopular.
4. They are expensive.
5. Their many rooms seem useless.
6. Large kitchens appear inconvenient.
7. Too much space is wasteful.
8. Today's small families would become unhappy.

SENTENCE PROBLEMS

This section deals with problems of sentences that are incomplete or that run together. You will find several ways of correcting these problems.

Sentence Fragments

4g A sentence fragment is an incomplete sentence.

See Phrase, p. 328
See Clause, p. 313

A sentence fragment may be a word, a phrase, or a dependent clause. In every case, a fragment needs more words to complete its meaning.

EXAMPLES *The rotten apple*
[What about the rotten apple? This fragment needs a predicate: *The rotten apple smelled awful.*]

Aimed at his heart
[What was aimed at his heart? This fragment needs a subject: *Cupid's arrow was aimed at his heart.*]

If she sings as well tomorrow
[This fragment is an incomplete statement. It fails to tell what will happen tomorrow if she sings as well. It needs an independent clause to complete it: *If she sings as well tomorrow, the concert will be a success.*]

EXERCISE 15 Number a sheet of paper 1–10. The following groups of words contain some complete sentences and some sentence fragments. Next to each number write *S* if the group of words is a sentence or *F* if the group of words is a fragment.

EXAMPLE Until we hear from them

F

1. Into a terrible problem
2. The lawyers argued in vain
3. Customers walked out
4. When the judge decided
5. Because it seemed fair to all sides
6. The store had charged too much for the stove
7. As it was being delivered
8. The truckers went on strike
9. Left out on the street
10. No power was available

Learn to recognize a sentence fragment. Then learn how to correct it.

The two most common kinds of sentence fragments are the phrase fragment and the dependent clause fragment.

Examples of the phrase used as a sentence fragment:

In a minute
[This prepositional phrase needs both a subject and a predicate to make it into a complete sentence: *The bus will come in a minute.*]

The lightning bolt
[This noun phrase could be the complete subject of a sentence. However, it needs a predicate to make a complete sentence: *The lightning bolt struck a tree.*]

Could have been damaged
[This verb phrase might be the predicate in a sentence. However, the subject is missing: *The house could have been damaged.*]

EXERCISE 16 Following are ten sentence fragments that are phrases. On a sheet of paper, rewrite each fragment so that it is made into a complete sentence.

EXAMPLE The silver candlesticks

The silver candlesticks were polished with care.

1. Had escaped from prison
2. In the good bishop's home
3. Had a simple supper together
4. Went to bed before midnight
5. Gone in the early morning
6. The missing silver candlesticks
7. Caught by the police
8. Brought back to the bishop's home
9. In their hands the missing candlesticks
10. Had given them to him last night

Examples of the dependent clause as a sentence fragment:

> *When you go to the post office*
> [Although this sentence fragment has a subject and a predicate, it is incomplete. It is a dependent clause that needs an independent clause to complete its meaning: *When you go to the post office, please buy some stamps.*]
>
> *Because Dale is never late*
> [This dependent clause needs an independent clause to make it a complete sentence: *Because Dale is never late, I think my watch is wrong.*]

EXERCISE 17 The following are ten sentence fragments that are dependent clauses. On a sheet of paper, rewrite each clause to make it a complete sentence. Do this by adding an independent clause.

EXAMPLE If you put a coin in the slot

You will get an apple if you put a coin in the slot.

1. Although Andy knows the way
2. When you reach Water Avenue
3. As the road bends to the right
4. Before you reach the bridge
5. If you miss the turn-off at the bridge
6. While they are repairing the bridge
7. Just as you pass Stem's apple orchard
8. Although he owns the property
9. Where they sell apples at the roadside
10. When you smell the odor of sweet apple cider

Run-on Sentences

4h A run-on sentence is two or more sentences incorrectly joined.

EXAMPLE Donny knew he was about to fall the ledge was not wide enough to hold him.

At least two methods can be used to correct run-on sentences.

Method 1: A run-on sentence may need to be split into separate sentences.

EXAMPLES Harriet put water in her car's radiator and air in its tires then she drove away.
[Run-on sentence]

Harriet put water in her car's radiator and air in its tires. Then she drove away.
[Correct separate sentences]

Method 2: A run-on sentence may be made into a compound sentence by adding a comma and a coordinating conjunction. At other times a run-on sentence may be made into a complex sentence by adding only a subordinating conjunction.

EXAMPLES The mechanic saw her he rushed out of the garage.
[Run-on sentence]

The mechanic saw her, and he rushed out of the garage.
Or
The mechanic saw her as he rushed out of the garage.
[Correct sentences]

EXERCISE 18 The following sentences are run-on sentences. Rewrite each sentence on a sheet of paper. Correct each one by using one of the two methods.

EXAMPLE Hazel saw water leaking through the ceiling she yelled upstairs.

Hazel saw water leaking from the ceiling. She yelled upstairs.

1. Most of the forms of punishment in early America were different from what they are now they were harsher in many ways.
2. Serious crimes were usually punished by death less serious ones were dealt with in a number of ways.
3. Whipping was used in certain cases sometimes a person was whipped in public as an example for others to remember.
4. Sometimes an offender was placed in the town square in stocks these were boards with holes that held the wrists or ankles.
5. A person in the stocks could not hide from the view of other townspeople even dogs or other stray animals were better off than a person in the stocks.
6. A petty thief might have to wear a sign for a month telling everyone of the crime a person who used bad language might have a stick put in his or her mouth like the bit in a horse's mouth.

REVIEW EXERCISE A **Subject and Predicate**

Number a sheet of paper 1–10. Write the simple subject and the simple predicate of each of the following sentences. Put *S* over the simple subject and *V* over the verb. For sentences with compound subjects or predicates, write all of the simple subjects or verbs.

EXAMPLE Many people in colonial America believed in the evil power of witches.

1. In 1692, fear of witches grew strong in Salem, Massachusetts.
2. Some young girls heard stories of witchcraft.
3. The girls fell to the ground and shouted loudly.
4. Their explanation was frightening.
5. Demons were sticking pins in them.
6. The girls and their parents accused many people in Salem of witchcraft.
7. A committee arrested and tried several hundred persons.
8. Several people were hanged.
9. Others escaped hanging by falsely admitting their guilt.
10. Terror walked the streets of Salem.

REVIEW EXERCISE B **Clauses**

Number a sheet of paper 1–15. Identify each of the following as an independent clause *I,* a dependent clause *D,* or a phrase *Ph.*

EXAMPLE in the spring

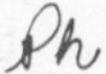

1. When the weather is clear and cold
2. Because he was very rich
3. After a game
4. Damon always eats early
5. Although bright and alert

6. He was small
7. During lunch
8. If no one catches you
9. When a jet plane takes off
10. Pass the salt, please
11. Living in a jungle
12. Look at the word list
13. Because of his bicycle
14. Oranges rot in rain
15. Stop

REVIEW EXERCISE C Sentence Structure

Number a sheet of paper 1–10. Identify each of the following sentences as simple *S*, complex *Cx*, or compound *C*.

EXAMPLE When the bough breaks, the baby will fall.

Cx

1. In 1913, part of America became a dust bowl.
2. Dry weather and strong winds created the dust bowl.
3. When a young boy became confused on the way home from school, the child was buried in dust.
4. Many farmers left their farms, and thousands of them moved to California.
5. When buffalo grazed on the plains, there had not been bad dust storms.
6. Buffalo ate the long grass, but they left the grass plants in the soil.
7. The plants held the soil even in wind storms.

8. As farmers plowed the land, they destroyed the grass.
9. The soil blew away when dry weather combined with strong wind.
10. Dust covered the land in Kansas, Oklahoma, and parts of Colorado.

REVIEW EXERCISE D Sentence Patterns

Number a sheet of paper 1–15. Label each sentence as Pattern 1 (S-V), Pattern 2 (S-V-O), Pattern 2a (S-V-IO-DO), or Pattern 3 (S-LV-SC).

EXAMPLE Washington Irving was an American writer.

Pattern 3 (S-LV-SC)

1. Washington Irving gave Americans the story of Rip Van Winkle.
2. Rip's wife was sharp-tongued and quick-tempered.
3. Rip took his gun and his dog to the Catskill Mountains.
4. He met some mysterious men.
5. They gave him a strong drink.
6. The drink put Rip to sleep for twenty years.
7. Finally something awakened him.
8. Thick rust appeared on his gun.
9. His beard had grown long and white.
10. He was a very old man.
11. Village children gave him frightened stares.
12. Even Rip's dog did not recognize him.
13. Rip was also frightened and confused.

14. A picture of George Washington and a flag with thirteen stars had replaced a picture of King George of England.
15. Rip Van Winkle had slept through the American Revolution.

REVIEW EXERCISE E Purposes of Sentences

On a sheet of paper, write four sentences about each of the following topics. The first sentence should be declarative, the second interrogative, the third imperative, and the fourth exclamatory. Identify the purpose of each sentence.

EXAMPLE dogs

Dogs are friendly beasts.
declarative

Do you like dogs?
interrogative

Don't pet strange dogs.
imperative

Look out for that yellow dog!
exclamatory

1. a dime
2. candy
3. mud
4. windows

REVIEW EXERCISE F Fragments

Number a sheet of paper 1–10. For each of the following word groups that is a complete sentence, write *complete*. For each fragment, add an independent clause to make a complete sentence.

EXAMPLE Sitting in the window

The girl felt very happy sitting in the window.

1. My uncle laughed at me when I ran from a cow
2. Because I had not seen a cow before
3. Cows on television, of course, are not frightening.
4. Quietly eating in a large field
5. As I was returning from a fishing trip
6. Having caught a large fish
7. One large cow moved slowly across the field
8. If the cow had stood still
9. That it only wanted to be friendly
10. I admit my fear

REVIEW EXERCISE G Run-on Sentences

One of each of the following groups of words is a run-on sentence. The other group of words is a correct sentence. Number a sheet of paper 1–5. Rewrite each run-on sentence correctly.

EXAMPLE A. A black cat may bring bad luck.
B. Don't let a black cat cross your path it may bring bad luck.

Don't let a black cat cross your path. It may bring bad luck.

1. A. The word *steward* originally meant the sty ward or the keeper of the pig sty.
   B. A steward now usually takes care of people he does not take care of pigs.
2. A. The interviewer talked for a few minutes then she got up and left the room.
   B. Some television stations send out interviewers to talk to people on the street.
3. A. The dentist, the plumber, and the electrician all use pliers.
   B. The electrician grabbed his pliers he wanted to disconnect the dangerous wires.
4. A. If the weatherman is a woman, will she be called a meteorologist?
   B. That woman studies the weather she is called a meteorologist.
5. A. The navigator had no trouble finding Hawaii he flew the plane directly there.
   B. Good navigators always know the direction they are going.

UNIT TWO

COMPOSITION

Paragraphs
Guidelines for Writing

CHAPTER

5

PARAGRAPHS

Sometimes you can write about an idea in one sentence. If you want to tell more about the idea, however, you will need to write several sentences. Together these sentences make up a *paragraph.*

The first sentence in each paragraph is indented a few spaces in from the left margin. Many paragraphs state their main idea in the first sentence. The other sentences in the paragraph develop that one idea.

DEVELOPING PARAGRAPHS

5a A paragraph is a series of sentences that tell about a single idea, description, or action.

Use a paragraph to develop a single idea called the *topic.* The idea might be an opinion you hold. For example, you might believe that school has many advantages. You want to write that school does have benefits. Your first sentence should state that idea clearly. Then the following sentences that make up the paragraph should be about the same idea.

EXAMPLE School provides many benefits. It offers a storehouse of ideas and a place where students can learn from the past. It is a place to meet people and make new friends. It gives young people a place to organize their lives outside their homes. It provides a center for social activity. Anything from athletic events to dances may be a part of school life.

5b State the main idea of a paragraph in a topic sentence.

Begin a paragraph by stating your main idea in the first sentence. This is the *topic sentence.* Think what you want to say. Then write your thought in the topic sentence.

Do you want to tell about an experience? Name that experience in the topic sentence. Then add details about that experience in the following sentences in the paragraph.

Do you want to express an idea or an opinion? State the idea or opinion in the topic sentence. Then give more details to support your idea or opinion in the rest of the sentences in the paragraph.

Following is an example of a paragraph giving the writer's idea. Note that the major point is made in the first sentence. This is the topic sentence.

The Model T Ford revolutionized American automobile travel. The car was inexpensive. In 1925 the price was $260. The low price made it possible for many people to buy cars for the first time. A pick-up truck attachment made it an all-purpose vehicle. Farmers and laborers could use it to haul crops or tools. This inexpensive transportation changed American habits of travel.

EXERCISE 1 Number a sheet of paper 1, 2, and 3 to stand for the following paragraphs. Each paragraph lacks a topic sentence. Following the paragraphs, there are six possible topic sentences. Choose the best topic sentence for each paragraph. Write the topic sentence next to the number of the paragraph.

1. (Topic sentence missing.) If the temperature goes below 21° C, the fish slow down. They seem tired. Often they become sick. If the temperature goes above 32° C, the fish are overactive. They seem to do everything too fast. In this heat, tropical fish live quickly. They often die quickly, too.
2. (Topic sentence missing.) Releasing air allows the submarine to submerge. Air is forced out of its ballast tanks. Air is also used to keep the ship level and balanced in the water. Forced air blows water from one tank to another. Sometimes the water is simply blown out to sea. When it is time to surface, compressed air is forced into tanks of water. The water makes room for the air, and the ship rises.
3. (Topic sentence missing.) Roads of dirt became dust trails in dry weather. In wet weather,

they turned to deep mud. Ruts and holes broke many a wheel or axle. It was nearly impossible to go faster than 20 miles per hour. Every hundred miles or so one could expect to have a tire blow out.

1. Americans could buy cheap cars.
2. Submarines can submerge or surface in most water.
3. Temperature control is important in a tropical fish aquarium.
4. Tropical fish get sick if the water temperature is too low.
5. The use of air is very important in a submarine.
6. Traveling in the American countryside by automobile in the early 1900's was a very serious problem.

5c Keep every sentence in a paragraph on the topic.

When you write a paragraph, make each sentence say something about the topic.

Study the two following paragraphs. Paragraph A includes only sentences that tell about its topic. Paragraph B contains one sentence that is not about its topic. Can you find the misplaced sentence in Paragraph B?

A. Cotton was the main crop grown in the South from 1815 to 1860. In 1820 the cotton crop was 72 million kilograms. By 1860 it reached about one billion kilograms. At that time, two-thirds of all exports of the United States was raw cotton or cotton goods. Any

Southerner who wanted to succeed in those times had to think of cotton first.

B. Cotton has been an important crop in the South for nearly two hundred years. Until the Civil War in the 1860's, it was the main source of income. After that war, its importance lessened somewhat. The textile mills in New England wove cotton cloth. Cotton continues to be vital to the South's economy.

The misplaced sentence in Paragraph B is the next-to-last sentence: *The textile mills in New England wove cotton cloth.* It does not refer to the topic.

EXERCISE 2 Number a sheet of paper 1–3. One of the sentences in each of the following three paragraphs does not belong in the paragraph. Next to each number, write the sentence that does not belong in the paragraph.

EXAMPLE

The common toad catches food with its tongue. The tongue of a full-grown toad may be more than an inch long. The toad can flick its tongue very fast. It is difficult to see. It is not true that a toad causes warts. The tongue is sticky and catches the toad's food.

It is not true that a toad causes warts.

1. Mark Twain wrote several stories about life in America. *Roughing It* and *Life on the Missis-*

sippi are both set in the heartland of this country. Twain was one of America's greatest writers. Two of his other well-known writings about America are *Tom Sawyer* and *Huckleberry Finn.*

2. A turtle lives longer than any other animal of its kind. One turtle in captivity is known to have lived more than 150 years. The shell of a turtle is its backbone. The common box turtle found in America often lives more than 100 years. Many other kinds live for more than 50 years.

3. All turtles lay eggs. Some land turtles dig nests in the soft ground. Others lay eggs in the soft wood of a rotting log. Their eggs, warmed by the sun, hatch in about two months. The green sea turtle comes ashore to lay her eggs in the sand. Seagulls feed on baby turtles whose shells are still soft.

5d Develop a paragraph with details, examples, and reasons.

The following paragraph is developed through the use of details.

> A coral reef in the tropical sea can be the feeding ground for thousands of fish. Colorful butterfly fish nibble at coral plants. Grazing nearby are angelfish and different kinds of parrot fish. The beaklike mouths of parrot fish, well-shaped for their work, break off bits of coral to eat. The big-eyed squirrel fish seem to hang motionless in the water over a coral

> hump. They stare for long minutes at spots ahead of them. Elsewhere the blue and green wrasse fish make their way among the branches of coral and the other feeding fish. The fish of countless shapes, colors, and sizes move about in a seemingly endless search for food.

The opening sentence serves as the topic sentence. The remaining sentences within the paragraph provide details related to the topic.

The following paragraph is developed through the use of examples. Each example is a piece of information that helps explain or describe a main point.

> The Australian frilled lizard has a special way of frightening off its enemies. When approached, it rears on its hind legs. It spreads out a frill on each side of its neck. This frill fans out as much as 23 or 25 centimeters across. The lizard also opens its jaws wide and lets out a loud hissing sound.

The first sentence is the topic sentence. Every other sentence gives an example that supports the topic.

Examples should help make clear what the main topic is about.

> People use leather in a variety of ways. Most leather is used to make shoes. However, leather is also used in handbags, belts, gloves, and other articles of clothing. Leather is used to cover furniture. It also covers many kinds of balls used in sports.

Still another way of developing a paragraph is by giving reasons. If you state an opinion in the topic sentence, support that opinion with reasons. The following paragraph is developed by listing reasons to support the topic.

> Bicycle paths should be laid out wherever cars are permitted to go. This act would cut down on the use of fuel. It would reduce the problem of pollution of the air. It would save money, because bicycles cost less to buy and run. It would probably save lives, too, because not many people have been killed by being run over by a bicycle.

EXERCISE 3 Four topic sentences are printed here. Choose one sentence and fill in the blank. Then write a paragraph, using the sentence as your topic sentence. Write the rest of your sentences in the paragraph to supply details, examples, or reasons to support your topic sentence.

1. My day at ______ was filled with unexpected events.
2. ______ is the most thoughtful person I know.
3. If you know a harder job than ______, I hope you keep it to yourself.
4. One of the best sports to play is ______.

5e A paragraph may be organized by time.

Events happen at certain times. The sun rises in the morning. People move about and do things during the day. The sun sets in the evening. These and other events happen in a certain order, one after another.

Usually you will find it is a good idea to describe events in a paragraph in the order they happen. Here is an example of a paragraph organized by time.

> The accident happened faster than the driver realized. At one moment the road ahead was clear. Then suddenly there loomed before her a lumbering, grey monster. She jammed her foot on the brakes without thinking. At the same time, she spun the steering wheel to the left. In an instant she felt the sickening, uncontrolled skid of the tires. She clenched her eyes, expecting to feel the smash of the car. Finally the car swerved through a large puddle of muddy water and came to rest completely turned around.

Each event in the accident described above happens in time. Notice the words that help to show the relationship of the events in time.

At one moment . . .
Then . . .
At the same time . . .
In an instant . . .
Finally . . .

EXERCISE 4 The events in the following paragraph are out of order in time. Only the first sentence is in its right order. On a sheet of paper copy the sentences in the order in which the events happened. Look for word clues that will help you find the order of the events.

> (1) There was never a dull moment during the party Ned gave for Emily. (2) After the

games, Ned made a little speech. (3) When she had been given all the presents, Emily opened them one at a time. (4) First, we played some crazy games. (5) After Ned finished, everyone gave Emily her presents. (6) Finally, we had cake and ice cream.

EXERCISE 5 Select one of the following four topics as a topic sentence. Write a short paragraph of four or five sentences. Organize your paragraph by time. Keep the events in their right order.

1. The life cycle of a butterfly makes a fascinating study.
2. There is only one way to cook scrambled eggs just right.
3. Making cement is easier than you think.
4. Papier-mâché sounds fancy, but it is really simple material to use.

5f A paragraph may be organized by space.

When you describe a place, you can organize the details of the paragraph according to space. Describe in the sentences where each object is in relation to the other objects in the place.

EXAMPLE

Jane was in trouble. She could see that. To her left the army ants swarmed nearer and nearer. To her right the lion lay waiting, hidden behind a screen of twisted vines. And right in front of her lay the brown ooze of quicksand. The only way to go was back, into the tangle of the jungle through which she had just struggled. But to go back down that hidden twisted path—if she could find it again—would be to go back toward the kidnappers who were chasing her.

EXERCISE 6 Select one of the following four topics as a topic sentence. Write a short paragraph of four or five sentences. Organize the paragraph by space.

1. This is the way to set a place for dinner.
2. A soccer field is laid out for playing the game.
3. Gymnastics equipment is made up of several special pieces.
4. The dashboard of our car is set up for the ease and convenience of the driver.

5g A paragraph is used to show the words of a new speaker.

See Punctuation, pp. 236-237

When you write quotations, begin each person's speech with a new paragraph. The following example shows how the words of each new speaker begin a new paragraph.

> Tom wheeled suddenly and said, "Why, it's you, Ben! I warn't noticing."
>
> "Say—I'm going in a-swimming, I am. Don't you wish you could? But of course you'd druther *work*—wouldn't you? Course you would!"
>
> Tom contemplated the boy a bit, and said: "What do you call work?"
>
> "Why, ain't *that* work?"
>
> Tom resumed his whitewashing, and answered carelessly: "Well, maybe it is, and maybe it ain't. All I know is, it suits Tom Sawyer." (Mark Twain, *Tom Sawyer*)

REVIEW EXERCISE A Topic Sentence

Each of the following groups of sentences is a scrambled paragraph. Decide on the correct order of the sentences. Look for the topic sentence, the sentence that states the topic of the whole paragraph. Number a sheet of paper 1–3. After each number, write the letter of the topic sentence for the paragraph.

Paragraph 1

A. This device protects buildings from damage by lightning.
B. Franklin put a pointed iron rod on the roof of his house.
C. He extended the rod five feet into the moist ground.
D. In 1752, Benjamin Franklin built the first lightning rod.
E. The metal rod in the moist earth conducted a lightning flash into the earth.

Paragraph 2

A. It was a clubhouse for the old men in town.
B. It was also a meeting place for friends and neighbors.
C. The old country store was more than a store.
D. Parents left their children at the store while they visited the blacksmith or the dentist.
E. It was a bank, a post office, and a baby-sitting service.

Paragraph 3

A. Peddlers traveled through forests and over mountains in the growing nation.
B. They carried their wares in trunks.

C. The trunks often became heavier as they sold their goods.
D. Since money was scarce, they traded their goods for honey, furs, or homemade wooden articles.
E. The Yankee peddler was for a long time one of America's most important business people.

REVIEW EXERCISE B Paragraph Unity

Number a sheet of paper 1–5. One of the sentences following each topic sentence is not closely related to the topic sentence. Write the letter of the sentence that does not belong with the topic.

1. When everything in a paragraph is related to the main idea, the paragraph has unity.
   A. In a unified paragraph every sentence backs up or makes clear the main idea.
   B. Indent the first sentence to mark off a paragraph.
   C. Nothing in the paragraph should take the reader's mind away from the main idea.
2. Many poor boys have grown up to become important men in America.
   A. Benjamin Franklin had only enough money for a loaf of bread when he first entered Philadelphia, where he later became wealthy and famous.
   B. Abraham Lincoln was born in a log cabin, but he later became president of the United States.
   C. Franklin Roosevelt was the son of rich parents, but he had to overcome a crippling illness before he became president.

D. The adventure story writer Jack London had to leave school when he was twelve because of his mother's poverty.

3. Colonial schools were different from schools of today.
   A. Colonial children went to school only two or three months each year.
   B. Colonial children were taught the alphabet, and then learned to read and to write, just as children do today.
   C. Schools had few books and little other equipment.
   D. Often the teachers in colonial schools had not gone to school long themselves.
4. Some workers face great dangers to their health and safety.
   A. A swimmer is foolish to endanger his life by swimming alone.
   B. Workers in some paint factories handle white lead, a dangerous poison.
   C. Coal miners run the risk of mine cave-ins and floods.
   D. A traffic police officer certainly must worry about being hit by a car or a bus.
   E. Men and women in high-wire circus acts take risks that thrill and frighten everyone.
5. It is easy and safe to swing on a birch tree.
   A. Robert Frost wrote a poem about swinging called "Birches."
   B. The climber should first find a tall tree.
   C. The birch tree will bend easily, but will not break easily.
   D. The climber should climb the tree slowly.
   E. As the tree bends, the climber swings safely and easily back to earth.

REVIEW EXERCISE C Methods of Development

Number a sheet of paper 1–5. Tell how you would develop each of the following topic sentences, by details, examples, or reasons, by time, or by space.

EXAMPLE Fruit is a good choice for dessert.
by reasons

1. I hate to shop for clothes.
2. It is easy to recognize a glutton.
3. Putting on shoes (or a jacket, or a hat) is not an easy matter.
4. There are three important steps in eating a hot dog.
5. When I stepped into the bakery, I just looked around.

REVIEW EXERCISE D Paragraph and Word List

Choose one of the topic sentences in Exercise C. Using the method of development that you have chosen for it, write a paragraph on the topic.

CHAPTER

6

GUIDELINES FOR WRITING

Many thousands of years ago—before books were written—people tried to write about their experiences and their ideas. But their writing was limited. They could use only pictures. They drew crude pictures of animals and objects they saw around them. They had no way of drawing a picture of a sound, a taste, an idea, or a feeling.

If some of those ancient people were able to come back to life to learn your system of writing, they would be amazed. Your writing is not restricted to showing just the things around you. You can write about anything you can talk about or think about. You can write about what any of your senses let you know about. You can write about ideas and feelings. You can use sentences to express ideas and feelings. You can combine your sentences into paragraphs.

Words in sentences and sentences in paragraphs make up a *composition*. When you write about a topic in a composition, you are putting to use most of the skills of English.

CHOOSING YOUR TOPIC AND YOUR AUDIENCE

6a Write about what you know.

To get started in writing, choose a subject you know well. You probably know yourself better than you know anything else. Writing about yourself is writing about what you know best.

When you choose to write about yourself, be careful not to put too much in your writing. You will want to make choices. Think of answers to these questions: *"What has happened to me that I can tell others?" "What words can I use?" "How can I put those words together?"*

Even if you write about something other than yourself, you will need to know about it. Only by knowing about it will you write well about it.

EXERCISE 1 Choose one of the following topics. Make a list of the things that happened to you.

1. The time I got cheated
2. My most exciting ride
3. The best TV show I ever saw
4. The best place I know
5. My most embarrassing moment
6. My luckiest day
7. My biggest surprise

8. The time I was really scared
9. The day I earned the most money
10. My worst meal

EXERCISE 2 Study the list of things you wrote for Exercise 1. If necessary, rearrange them in the order they happened. Write a short composition of at least one paragraph telling about the experience you chose.

6b Choose a topic to suit your audience.

You will also find it easier to write if you know who will read your writing. Writers call this "knowing the audience." This means having certain people in mind as you write. Knowing who the reader will be as you write is similar to knowing who your listener is while you talk. Knowing your reader will help you choose a topic that will interest him or her.

EXERCISE 3 You might choose to write about some of the following topics to anyone you have met. Other topics you would write about only to a close friend. Number a sheet of paper 1–8. Next to each number, write *F* if you would write about the topic only to a close friend. If you would write about the topic to anyone you know, put *A*.

1. An auto accident you saw
2. A serious argument you had with a friend
3. A valuable gift you received
4. The time you forgot to study for a test
5. A serious fire in your neighborhood
6. A special note you received from a close friend

7. Some money you found
8. A broken promise

EXERCISE 4 Write a short composition of at least one paragraph about one of the topics in Exercise 3. List the audience you have chosen.

ORGANIZING YOUR WRITING

Organizing your writing means thinking ahead. It means thinking about what you want to say and the people you want to say it to.

Put yourself in the place of your reader. Your reader needs to know what your topic is. Your reader needs to know at the start the limits of your topic.

6c Limit the topic you choose to write about.

As soon as you have chosen a topic, think about its size. Most topics that you first think of may be too broad to write about in a short composition.

For example, the topic "Accidents in the Home" is too broad for a short composition because there are so many kinds of accidents. *Limit* the topic or make it smaller to deal with one special accident. "The Time I Slashed My Finger" would be a limited topic.

Other examples of limited topics are these:

BROAD TOPIC	LIMITED TOPIC
Desserts	The best dessert I ever tasted
Clothing	My favorite shoes
Sports	The end of a perfect game

EXERCISE 5 In the following list are five limited topics and five topics too broad to write about in a short composition. Make two columns on a sheet of paper. List the broad topics in the left-hand column. List the limited topics in the right-hand column.

Weather in our state	Polluting the rivers
The sweetest taste I know	Food for all tastes
Strange objects on a riverbank	What a barometer tells us
A simple dance step	Working at the post office
The junk I bought	History of the dance

6d Relate events in the order they happened.

Help your reader understand what you write about by keeping events in order. If you tell about an experience you have had, start at the beginning. For example, you might tell about an accident at home. Suppose you spilled some paint while helping to paint a room at home. You plan to write about your experience.

Begin by making a list of things that happened. Here is a possible list.

1. set up a stepladder
2. spread newspapers on the floor
3. moved furniture
4. stirred the paint
5. dipped in the paint brush
6. climbed the ladder
7. started to paint
8. tipped over the paint can with my knee
9. spilled paint on the floor and on myself
10. cleaned up most of the paint

Some of the events in this list may be out of order. Some may even be missing. You can easily change the list by writing down the numbers in a new order. Number 3 might come before Number 2, for instance. You usually spread newspapers *after* you move furniture. This kind of list helps you relate events in order. The order will help your reader see what happened.

EXERCISE 6 Most of the following events in an accident are out of order. Only the first and last event are in order. On a sheet of paper, write these events in the order they most likely happened.

> I stepped off the curb when the light turned green for me.
> The truckdriver jammed on the brakes.
> The truckdriver opened the door and got out.
> I jumped back toward the curb.
> A truck came rushing at me.
> The truck swerved away to avoid hitting me.
> The truck's brakes made a loud noise, and the tires squealed in a skid.
> I felt scared, but no one was hurt.

EXERCISE 7 Choose one of the following topics. Make a list of events that happened. Make sure your list is in the correct order.

1. An accident
2. A fight
3. A wrongdoing
4. An unusual discovery
5. A happy event

6e Tell where events happened.

Sometimes in your writing you may forget to tell where an event happened. When you forget to tell about the place, your reader may find it hard to "see" what you are writing about.

The place where events happen is called the *setting*. Give the setting when you write about an experience.

EXERCISE 8 Write a short composition of one paragraph telling about the place where you had an unusual experience. Choose an experience from the list in Exercise 1 on page 122, or think of another experience you might write about.

6f Tie events together by causes and effects.

Your experiences are made up of events that are caused by something. These causes and effects, or results, are links in a chain of your experience. An accident, for example, is the result of something that you usually can tell about. Perhaps you or someone else was careless. If you have had a fall, this accident may have been caused by your tripping over an obstacle. To help your writing make sense, tell about the cause of an event as well as the event itself.

EXERCISE 9 Following are two lists. The first list includes causes. The second list includes events. These events are effects of the causes. Number a sheet of paper 1–5. Match the causes and effects. Next to each number, write the cause, then write the effect.

CAUSES	EFFECTS
1. the firing of a gun	the shell breaks
2. the temperature drops below 0° C	the animal moves quickly
3. a raw egg is dropped on the floor	the sound of an explosion
4. a musician taps a key on the piano	water freezes
5. someone accidentally steps on the tail of a cat	a musical note is heard

Remember to tie together important events by showing their causes and by keeping them in order of time and place.

See Adverb; p. 311; Preposition, p. 329; Conjunction, p. 316

Certain connecting words or phrases help show how causes and effects are related. *Connectors* are conjunctions, adverbs, or prepositions. *Because* is a connecting word that is often used.

EXAMPLE The paint spilled *because* I hit the can with my knee.

Some other connecting words are *therefore, then, as a result of, since,* and *when.*

EXAMPLES *Since* she has enough money, she plans to buy the shoes.
As a result of Jim's fast lap, our team won the relay race.

EXERCISE 10 Write five complete sentences. Show in each a cause and an effect joined by a connecting word or phrase. You may use the causes and effects listed in Exercise 9.

CHOOSING YOUR WORDS

6g Use words and phrases that appeal to the senses.

Words that appeal to the senses are called *sensory words.*

EXAMPLES *shiny, wet* pavement
boxlike houses
jagged fingernail
strong smell of onions
tangy taste of grapefruit
slapping of the *windblown* flag

These examples appeal to several of the five senses: sight, hearing, touch, taste, and smell. When writing about your experiences, use sensory words and phrases that appeal to your reader's five senses.

EXERCISE 11 Following is a list of words that appeal to the senses. On a sheet of paper, make five columns across the top. Write one of the senses as a heading for each column: Sight, Hearing, Touch, Taste, Smell. Under each heading write the words from the list that appeal to that sense. For example, the word *jingle* goes under *Hearing* because it appeals to the ear. Some words appeal to more than one sense. You may put them under either heading.

sizzle	fiery	rough
bitter	perfume	caramel
pink	satin	diamond
gurgle	aromatic	pebbly
curved	sour	angular
thump	thud	puckery

6h Use comparisons in your descriptions.

Comparisons show how people are like other people or how one thing is like another. Comparisons show how things are similar. A good comparison helps to describe a person or thing.

EXAMPLES

SIMPLE DESCRIPTION The field was muddy.
COMPARISON The field looked like a muddy carpet.

SIMPLE DESCRIPTION The bird flew fast.
COMPARISON The bird flew as fast as a tiny jet fighter.

These comparisons relate one thing to another. The thing being described and the thing compared to it are similar. They are not the same, of course. However, they are alike in certain ways. The ways they are alike help make it easier for your reader to understand the description.

EXERCISE 12 List A contains objects or features. List B contains comparisons. Number a sheet of paper 1–6. Next to each number, write the item from List A. Next to it, write the best comparison from List B. The first one is done for you as an example.

EXAMPLE *a stylish hat like a crumpled lampshade*

LIST A	LIST B
1. a stylish hat	like a furious turkey
2. fat	as a faint star
3. distant	like a flat, blue mirror
4. a lake	like a crumpled lampshade
5. an angry politician	as a hundred trucks starting up
6. loud	as a stuffed pig

EXERCISE 13 The persons and objects listed here need comparisons to make their descriptions clearer to the reader. Write the items on a sheet of paper. Add your own comparison to each item to help describe it to your reader.

EXAMPLE a whistle

a whistle as shrill as a boiling teakettle

1. snow
2. a whisper
3. a wave
4. moonlight
5. a click
6. an eye
7. branches
8. mud
9. hard
10. a hiss

EXERCISE 14 Choose one of the following topics or choose a topic from Exercise 1 on page 122. Write a composition of one or two paragraphs. Include comparisons of persons or things you write about.

1. The best ride I ever had
2. The worst morning of my life
3. The worst game I ever saw
4. The best pet I ever had
5. The time I could hardly stop laughing
6. The time my friend could hardly stop laughing
7. My most frightening ride
8. The time I won the game
9. The time I lost the game
10. The time my (brother, sister, friend) got lost

6i Be specific by adding details, examples, or reasons.

Ideas often sound weak when they are expressed alone. They need support with specific details, examples, and reasons. Here is an example of a general idea without supporting details, examples, or reasons.

Mt. Whitmore Lodge is the best place for a vacation.

This statement expresses an opinion. However, there are no details, examples, or reasons to support it. The reader will probably not be convinced that the statement is true.

Here are some possible ways to make the statement stronger.

> Mt. Whitmore Lodge is the best place for a vacation. The air seems cleaner because of the altitude. The food has always been excellent. Also, it costs less than most other places in the country.

When you write an important idea or feeling, you should list some details, examples, or reasons that will support it.

EXERCISE 15 The following list offers some general statements of opinion. They need supporting details, examples, or reasons to make them stronger. Choose one of the statements. Write the complete statement on a sheet of paper. Then write down at least four details, examples, or reasons to support the statement.

1. *(name of a place to eat)* is the best place to eat out.
2. *(name of a comic strip)* is the best comic strip.
3. *(name of a comic strip)* is the worst comic strip.
4. *(name of a TV show)* is the best TV show.
5. The best time of life is when you are *(age)*.
6. The worst time of life is when you are *(age)*.

EXERCISE 16 Write about the topic you chose in Exercise 15. Use the supporting details, examples, and reasons you listed. Add more if you can. Write at least one paragraph.

WRITING LETTERS AND NOTES

6j Write friendly letters that please the receivers.

A letter to a relative or a friend is a kind of composition. You need to think about your audience, the receiver. You need to plan your writing so that it says what you really mean.

Follow the form shown on the next page.

182 Circle Drive
Racine, Wisconsin 53402
August 2, 1980

Dear Jody,

Thanks for asking me to visit you, but I can't this summer. Dad thinks we may go on a trip soon. He won't know for about two weeks, but that would be too late for me to make a trip over to the lake.

You and I can get together at Thanksgiving. Then we can set up something. You could come to our place for the New Year weekend.

I'll see you at Thanksgiving.

Your friend,

Jan

REVISING YOUR WRITING

6k Revise your writing to improve its effectiveness.

Once you have written a composition, you can make it better by revising it. One good way to revise is with the help of another person. Read your composition aloud to someone else. Ask your listener to think of words, phrases, and sentences that might be improved. Can you add words that will help your reader "see" more clearly what you describe? Do your phrases, clauses, and sentences state just what you mean? Could they be made more direct? Have you tied together your points in time and place? Do you tell about the causes of events?

Have you also supported your general statements with details, examples, and reasons? Possibly you can add more facts that make clearer what you mean.

If you do not read your composition aloud to someone else, read it aloud to yourself. Doing this will sometimes reveal weak parts in your writing. You can then revise the weak parts.

6l Check the mechanics of your writing.

The final check of your composition should be to see that your mechanics are correct. Is your handwriting clear? Have you spelled words correctly? Do you have the right punctuation in the right places? Did you put capital letters on the right words? Check your composition against the Composition Checklist that follows. It will give you a guide for your own writing and will help you to correct any errors you may have overlooked.

COMPOSITION CHECKLIST

1. Do you know enough about your topic?
2. Do you know who your audience is?
3. Does your topic suit your audience?
4. Is your topic limited so that you can deal with it?
5. Have you organized the events according to time and place?

6. Have you used certain words and phrases that appeal to the audience?
7. Have you used comparisons?
8. Have you supported main ideas with details, examples, and reasons?
9. Does each paragraph develop a single idea or event?
10. Are your words, phrases, and sentences doing their best work?
11. Have you left any phrases or clauses separated from the complete sentences?
12. Have you checked the mechanics to the best of your ability?

REVIEW EXERCISE A Limiting the Topic

Write the headings *Broad* and *Limited* on a piece of paper. Put each topic in the following pairs of topics in one of the two columns.

EXAMPLE A. School sports
B. The neglected swimming team

Broad	Limited
School sports	The neglected swimming team

1. A. Our school
   B. The food in our school cafeteria
2. A. A fifty-five-mile-an-hour speed limit
   B. Driving rules in America
3. A. Trees
   B. Looking at a giant redwood tree

4. A. My summer vacation
   B. Two weeks at Camp Summerfun
5. A. The history of the circus in Hungary
   B. Trained bears in the Moscow circus

REVIEW EXERCISE B Methods of Organization

Number a sheet of paper 1–5. Next to each number identify the method of organization of the paragraph. Each paragraph is developed by examples, by time, or by cause and effect.

1. After capturing Fort Henry, General Grant moved on twelve miles to Fort Donelson. He and his men attacked the fort for three days. Finally, General Buchner asked for an armistice. When Grant said that he would continue fighting until Buchner gave in completely, Buchner surrendered the fort.
2. Gettysburg is an historic place in America. The battle fought there marked a turning point in the Civil War. Many soldiers from both sides of that war died at Gettysburg and are buried there. It was at Gettysburg that Lincoln gave his Gettysburg Address. In that famous speech he explained the main ideas of a democratic government.
3. To use Natural Glory Shampoo, first wet your hair. Then apply a small amount of the shampoo to your hair. Rub to a rich lather. Finally, rinse your hair until all the shampoo has been rinsed away. Enjoy the clean, shining beauty of your hair.

4. Forest ranger Miguel Torres had a serious problem. How could he stop the visitors who were writing their names on the trees and the granite boulders in the Tahoe National Forest? For Mr. Torres the answer was simple. He put visitors' books throughout the forest. Now visitors sign their names and write their messages in the books and leave the trees and rocks alone.
5. Many words in the English language have been borrowed from other languages. *Tattoo* is a Polynesian word; *seersucker* is Persian. *Chipmunk, moose, pecan,* and *squash* are all borrowed from Native American languages. These borrowings make English interesting and varied.

REVIEW EXERCISE C **Paragraph Organization**

The order of the sentences in the following paragraphs has been scrambled. On a sheet of paper, rewrite each paragraph, putting the sentences in correct order.

Paragraph 1

A. He will tell you about the car.
B. If the Zooper sounds like a good car, hurry to your Zooper dealer for more information.
C. He will also let you test-drive a Zooper.
D. After this, you will surely want to buy a Zooper.

Paragraph 2

A. In 1780, the first United States Patent Office was opened in New York City.
B. The patent showed this: When the hen left the hen house, a sign appeared saying, "I'm out. You may have my egg now."

C. It was rebuilt, though, and by 1870, 200,000 patents were on file, including one for a fancy hen house.
D. By 1836, 7,000 patents had been granted.
E. When the building burned in 1836, all of its records were destroyed.

Paragraph 3
A. On the one hundred-seventh story of a building in New York, two men finished their dinner.
B. They took a last look at the beautiful lights of New York and crowded into an elevator.
C. Somebody else pried the doors open and the passengers stepped out again.
D. The doors slipped shut.
E. The elevator did not move.
F. Somebody pushed the "down" button.
G. "So is New York," the waiter answered, looking down at the darkened view.
H. "The elevator is out," said one passenger to a waiter.

REVIEW EXERCISE D **Paragraphs**

Write a paragraph in which you describe someone you know well. Remember to have a single topic sentence and to have each sentence clearly relate to that topic sentence. Think also about your audience. Are you writing for a reader who has never seen the person you are describing or for someone who has not seen this person for several years or for someone who sees this person often? Try to use one comparison in your paragraph.

REVIEW EXERCISE E **Word List**

Review the following words.

cinnamon	satin
corduroy	spaghetti
gauze	suede
gristle	syrup
ketchup	taffeta
licorice	

On a sheet of paper, make a column for each of the five senses: *Sight, Sound, Touch, Taste, Smell.* Then list each of the words above under the sense to which the word appeals. Remember that a word may appeal to more than one sense.

UNIT THREE

USAGE

Using Parts of Speech
Common Confusions

CHAPTER

7

USING PARTS OF SPEECH

Read the two following sentences carefully. Which sentence is correct?

She doesn't have time.
She don't have time.

The answer to the question is a matter of *usage.*

Actually, the first sentence, *She doesn't have time,* is considered correct by most educated speakers of English. Even though the sentence *She don't have time* is easy to understand, it is not considered correct. It is "nonstandard." The standard form of the verb that goes with, or agrees with, *she* is *doesn't. Agreement* between subject and verb is just one of the matters of usage that is dealt with in this chapter. Others include active and passive verbs and the correct use of pronouns, adjectives, and adverbs.

AGREEMENT OF SUBJECTS AND VERBS

7a A verb must agree with its subject in number.

In the third person singular, present tense, regular verbs add **s** or **es.** In the other persons and in plurals, however, no ending is added for present tense. Only the infinitive form of the verb is used.

EXAMPLES

	SINGULAR	PLURAL
First Person (the one speaking)	I eat.	We eat.
Second Person (the one spoken to)	You eat.	You eat.
Third Person (the one spoken about)	He (or she or it) eats.	They eat.

Hint: If the plural noun ends in **s,** the verb usually does not end in **s.**

A pronoun can take the place of a noun. When it does, the verb must agree with it just as with a noun.

EXAMPLES The woman laughs.
She laughs.

Chipmunks run quickly.
They run quickly.

Certain nouns may be plural but take a singular verb because the nouns are singular in meaning.

EXAMPLES News *comes* every morning on station WEEZ.
Twenty cents *is* too much to pay.

EXERCISE 1 Number a sheet of paper 1–10. Write *S* next to each item that has a singular subject and verb. Write *P* next to each item that has a plural subject and verb.

EXAMPLE Summer disappears.

S

1. The leaves fall.
2. The clouds form.
3. Winter comes.
4. The storms rage.
5. The snow melts.
6. The weather turns warm.
7. The first leaf appears.
8. The sap runs.
9. Spring shows its clothing.
10. So the seasons turn.

EXERCISE 2 Rewrite each of the following items. Change each singular subject and verb to plural. Change each plural subject and verb to singular.

EXAMPLES Steers live on the range.

A steer lives on the range.

It survives the winter storms.

They survive the winter storms.

1. Cowboys round up the steers in the fall.
2. The cowboys ride in a large circular path.
3. They bring steers into a corral.
4. Sometimes a steer runs out of the corral.
5. A cowboy chases it.
6. He ropes it around the neck.
7. Steers lose weight with too much exercise.
8. Cowboys want them to stay in the corral.
9. A steer's muscle gets too tough from exercise.
10. The butcher likes to have tender meat.

7b A compound subject joined by the conjunction *and* usually takes a plural verb.

EXAMPLES Holly *and* Etta *make* wreaths at Christmas.
Harry *and* George *sell* the wreaths to the neighbors.

Even though each person is only one, together they make two. Two or more people or things, as a compound subject, take the plural form of the verb.

EXERCISE 3 Number a sheet of paper 1–10. Some of the following sentences have compound subjects. Choose the correct verb for each sentence. Write the verb next to the number of each sentence.

EXAMPLE Food and drink (makes/make) a meal.

make

1. Salt and grated cheese (go/goes) on the table at mealtime.
2. My father (sprinkle/sprinkles) cheese on his soup.
3. Many people (like/likes) pickles on hamburgers.
4. Sour cream and butter (taste/tastes) good on baked potatoes.
5. Dressing (add/adds) flavor to a salad.
6. Nuts and chocolate sauce (cover/covers) ice cream to make a sundae.
7. Cereal (seem/seems) dry without milk on it.
8. Peanuts and yogurt (make/makes) a good snack.
9. Applesauce (taste/tastes) good with pork.
10. Frosty yogurt (cover/covers) fruit for a tasty treat.

7c When compound subjects are joined by the conjunctions *or, nor, either . . . or,* or *neither . . . nor,* the verb agrees in number with the nearer subject.

EXAMPLES Vic *or* Abe *sleeps* on the porch. [Even though there are two persons as the subject, the verb is singular to agree with the nearer subject, *Abe.*]

Neither Jenny *nor* her friends *know* the combination. [*Friends* is nearer to the verb. Therefore, the verb is plural to agree with *friends,* not *Jenny.*]

> Only the members *or* their secretary *speaks* for the club. [Even though *members* is plural, the subject nearer the verb, *secretary,* is singular. The verb, therefore, is singular to agree with *secretary.*]

EXERCISE 4 Number a sheet of paper 1–5. Write the correct form of the verb next to each number.

> EXAMPLE Either a heatwave or a cold storm (seems/seem) to be our weather.
>
> *seems*

1. Either suntan oil or suntan lotion (helps/help) to darken a tan.
2. A raincoat or umbrella (keep/keeps) us dry in rainy weather.
3. Neither hurricanes nor tornadoes (stay/stays) in one spot.
4. A heater or blankets (is/are) helpful in cold weather.
5. Either the radio or newspapers (tell/tells) us about the weather.

7d When a group of words comes between the subject and the verb, the verb still agrees with the subject.

Sometimes a sentence will have words between the subject and the verb. In this kind of sentence, look carefully at the number of the subject. Decide whether the subject is singular or plural. Make sure the verb agrees with that number. Do not be fooled by the words that come between.

EXAMPLES The girls in the back of the room *make* a strong team.
[*Girls* is the subject, not *room*. Therefore, the verb *make* agrees with the subject.]

A carpenter using different tools *builds* structures out of wood.
[*Carpenter*, the subject, is singular. The verb *builds* agrees in number with *carpenter* rather than with *tools*.]

EXERCISE 5 Number a sheet of paper 1–8. Next to each number, write the correct choice of the verb in parentheses.

EXAMPLE One of our famous states (is/are) Texas.
is

1. The state of Texas (has/have) many attractions.
2. One of these (is/are) near Houston on the Gulf of Mexico.
3. The battleship U.S.S. *Texas,* famous in two world wars, (is/are) permanently berthed there.
4. Big Bend National Park, in the Chisos Mountains along the Rio Grande River, (was/were) established in 1944.

5. San Antonio, one of the state's major cities, (attracts/attract) thousands of tourists every year.
6. The Alamo, a site of famous battles, (stand/stands) in its busy streets.
7. Many Texans (know/knows) the cry, "Remember the Alamo!"
8. Texas, second largest of our states, (represents/represent) an important part of our nation's history.

7e Collective nouns may take singular or plural verbs.

Collective nouns name groups of persons or animals. Examples of collective nouns are *family, class, club, crowd, group, flock,* and *herd.* If the group is thought of as singular, the verb is singular. However, if the group is thought of as plural, the verb is plural.

EXAMPLES The *class argue* too much of the time.
[In this sentence, *class* is thought of as many separate members. Therefore, the verb is plural.]

The *class plans* to go tomorrow.
[Here the noun *class* is thought of as a single unit. Therefore, the verb is singular.]

7f Certain nouns and phrases that name a quantity may appear to be plural, but they take a singular verb.

EXAMPLES A *dozen* fills the basket to the top.
[A *dozen* is a single quantity.]

Ninety million miles is a long way to drift.
[*Ninety million miles* is a single distance.]

EXERCISE 6 Number a sheet of paper 1–5. Choose the correct form of the verb in each of the following sentences. Write your choice next to each number.

EXAMPLE A flock of pigeons (roosts/roost) every night on that building.
roosts

1. The herd of buffalo (wanders/wander) freely in the park.
2. Twenty thousand acres (is/are) enough territory for them.
3. The news of their arrival in the spring (brings/bring) interested ranchers.
4. The crowd of ranchers (discusses/discuss) whether anyone will start a fresh herd.
5. One dollar and sixty cents a kilogram (is/are) good payment for livestock.

7g A linking verb agrees with its subject.

EXAMPLES The quietest *time* of these days *is* the early morning hours.
[The linking verb *is* agrees with the subject, *time,* which is singular.]

The silliest *jokes seem* to make a comedy TV show popular.
[The linking verb *seem* agrees with the plural subject *jokes.*]

Here *are* your *coats.*
[Do not say or write *Here is your coats* or *Here's your coats. Coats* is the plural subject of the sentence.]

Where *are* my *books*?
[*Books* is the plural subject.]

EXERCISE 7 Number a sheet of paper 1–10. Next to each number write the correct form of the verb in parentheses.

EXAMPLE Where (is/are) the tickets for the show?

are

1. Geraldine Rizzo and her mother (was/were) late for the show.
2. There (is/are) not much time before it begins.
3. Where (is/are) those things?
4. Here (is/are) one of them.
5. The tickets for the show (was/were) under Geraldine's purse.
6. The other one of the tickets (was/were) next to the first one.
7. The cars in traffic (was/were) slower than ever.
8. Now where (is/are) an empty parking place?
9. (There's/There are) some empty ones across the street.
10. You mean our tickets for the show (was/were) only good for last week's show?

SPECIAL VERB PROBLEMS

Regular Verbs

Regular verbs form the *simple past tense* by adding **ed** to the infinitive, or base, form. Examples are *aim/aimed* and *work/worked.* To show an action that has already been completed in the past, regular verbs form the *present perfect* by using at least one helping verb and the *past participle* form of the main verb.

EXAMPLES	PRESENT TENSE	SIMPLE PAST	PRESENT PERFECT
	aim	aimed	have aimed
	work	worked	have worked

You *aim* the rifle carefully before shooting.
Jody *aimed* it at the bear after hearing the growl.
When you *have aimed* at the target, squeeze the trigger.

The Verb *Be*

The verb *be* has special forms in the present tense.

	SINGULAR	PLURAL
First Person	I am	we are
Second Person	you are	you are
Third Person	he / she / it } is	they are

Irregular Verbs

7h Irregular verbs usually form past tense by changing their spelling of the infinitive form.

EXAMPLES

PRESENT TENSE The preparations *begin* today for the fair.

SIMPLE PAST TENSE The preparations *began* yesterday for the fair.

PRESENT TENSE Marie *chooses* her clothes with extreme care.

SIMPLE PAST TENSE Marie *chose* that dress last week.

Most irregular verbs change form once again to show an action that has been completed, the present perfect.

EXAMPLES

PRESENT begin
SIMPLE PAST began
PRESENT PERFECT have begun

Today we *begin* the third house.
Yesterday we *began* the foundations.
Since last week we *have begun* four new houses.

These are three basic forms of commonly used irregular verbs.

PRESENT	SIMPLE PAST	PRESENT PERFECT
begin	began	have begun
break	broke	have broken
choose	chose	have chosen
do	did	have done
drive	drove	have driven
eat	ate	have eaten
fall	fell	have fallen
go	went	have gone
know	knew	have known
ride	rode	have ridden
ring	rang	have rung
see	saw	have seen
take	took	have taken
throw	threw	have thrown
wear	wore	have worn
write	wrote	have written

EXERCISE 8 Number a sheet of paper 1–8. Choose the correct form of the verb for each sentence. Write the verb next to each number.

EXAMPLE For years trucks (do/did) all the delivery of our company's product.

did

1. Truck drivers (begin/began) yesterday to prepare for a long haul.
2. When they started, some (choose/chose) to drive the southern route.
3. Those that went south said they (drive/have driven) that way before and like it best.
4. Others who have not (went/gone) the southern route know the central route better.

5. Many of them have (rode/ridden) it several times.
6. It (takes/have taken) them through Denver and Salt Lake City.
7. Truckers on the southern route have (saw/seen) plenty of hot desert.
8. The clothes they (wear/worn) are not heavy.

Active and Passive Verbs

A verb is in the *active voice* when it tells of action done by its subject. A verb is in the *passive voice* when the action is done to its subject.

See Subject, p. 331

EXAMPLES

ACTIVE VOICE Norton *drove* the bus.

PASSIVE VOICE The bus *was driven* by Norton. [The bus was being driven. It received the action.]

Hint: The passive voice uses a helping verb with a main verb.

EXERCISE 9 Copy each sentence below and underline the verb, then write *active* or *passive*. Three sentences have verbs in the passive voice.

EXAMPLE Mike was hit by a snowball.

Mike was hit by a snowball.
passive

1. Snow falls in cold climates.
2. The ground is covered by a white blanket.
3. The snow is made soft by warmer temperatures.
4. Soft snow sticks together.
5. Snowballs are made from sticky snow.
6. Mike forgot that fact.

SPECIAL PRONOUN PROBLEMS

Pronouns have a number of different forms, or *cases*.

7i The form of a personal pronoun depends on how it is used in a sentence.

(1) A pronoun used as the subject of the sentence is in the subjective case.

EXAMPLE *I* am 126 years old.

A pronoun used as the subject completer is also in the *subjective case.*

EXAMPLE Some people think I am *she.*

The forms of pronouns in informal speech often do not follow this rule. One hears the statements "*It's me,*" "*It's her,*" "*It's us,*" or other similar expressions. In writing, it is safe to follow the rule or change the wording from "*It's me*" to "*I am the one*" to avoid the construction.

(2) A pronoun used as the direct or indirect object in a sentence is in the objective case.

EXAMPLES Rex picked *me* up in his car.
He gave *me* a ride.

Here are the forms of the personal pronouns in the objective and subjective cases.

	SUBJECTIVE CASE		OBJECTIVE CASE	
	Singular	Plural	Singular	Plural
First Person	I	we	me	us
Second Person	you	you	you	you
Third Person	he		him	
	she	they	her	them
	it		it	

EXAMPLES *He* called *them.*
[*He* is singular in the subjective case. *Them* is plural in the objective case.]

We saw *her.*
[*We* is plural in the subjective case. *Her* is singular in the objective case.]

EXERCISE 10 Number a sheet of paper 1–6. Next to each number write the correct form of the pronoun in parentheses.

EXAMPLE It was (he/him) under the car.

1. Charlene and (she/her) have Mondays off.
2. In good weather they and (I/me) like to go to the park.
3. (We/Us) women sometimes take our cats.
4. Charlene's cat brings (us/we) mice and bugs.

5. (She/Her) and I like cats.
6. But (we/us) hate mice and bugs.

EXERCISE 11 Number a sheet of paper 1–8. Next to each number write correct forms of pronouns in parentheses to fill the blanks in the following sentences.

EXAMPLE Give that letter to ______. (I)

1. The captain chose Mel and ______ to lead the way. (I)
2. He suggested ______ and ______ come next. (he, you)
3. Then he directed ______ boys to follow behind. (we)
4. He said Mel and ______ should be careful. (I)
5. He showed ______ all how to walk on tiptoes. (we)
6. ______ and Mel started out. (he)
7. ______ boys came behind. (we)
8. I could hardly wait until ______ reached the marshmallow storehouse. (We)

7j The pronoun object of a preposition is in the objective case.

See Preposition, p. 329

A pronoun must be in the objective case when used as the object of a preposition.

EXAMPLES Come with *me*.
Joe came near *us*.

Sometimes a preposition has two or more objects. If one of the objects is a pronoun, it still is in the objective case.

EXAMPLES We heard about Jerry and *them*.
Sharon told it to him and *me*.

Hint: To be sure you have the pronoun in the right case when it and another word serve as objects of a preposition, follow these steps.

1. Remove the words between the preposition and the pronoun.
   We heard about Jerry and them.
2. Say the sentence without those words.
   We heard about . . . them.
3. If the pronoun is correct without the words, use it in the complete sentence.
   We heard about Jerry and them.

EXERCISE 12 Number a sheet of paper 1–12. Next to each number write the correct form of the pronoun in the parentheses.

EXAMPLE Ben Accardo gave his old baseballs to Ross and (I/me).

me

1. Ben used to play baseball with the gang and (I/me).
2. He gave tips on playing to Ross and (we/us).
3. We learned a lot from (he/him).

4. One day Alicia Lonberg wanted to play with Ben and (we/us).
5. Some of (we/us) wanted no part of that.
6. We thought no girl could keep up with Ben and (we/us).
7. But Ben told Alicia to practice hitting balls with Ross and (I/me).
8. She cracked some hard ones at Ross and (I/me).
9. When we chose up sides to play, Ross and I ended up on the same team with (she/her).
10. Alicia swung at nearly every ball pitched at (she/her).
11. She finally drove one between the first and second basemen; it got between (they/them) for a hit.
12. The next day our two teams argued whether Alicia should play with (they/them) or (we/us).

PROBLEMS WITH ADJECTIVES AND ADVERBS

See Adjective, p. 311; Adverb, p. 311;

It is important to keep in mind the difference between adjectives and adverbs.

See Linking Verb, p. 324

7k An adjective is used after a linking verb to modify the subject.

The adjective used after a linking verb refers back to the noun or pronoun that is the subject. On some occasions, an adverb will be incorrectly used in place of an adjective after a linking verb.

EXAMPLES

RIGHT The bell seems noisy.
[The adjective *noisy* modifies the subject by telling how the bell sounded.]

WRONG The bell seems too *noisily*.
[The adverb *noisily* cannot modify *bell* because *seems* is a linking verb.]

7l An adverb is used to modify an action verb.

RIGHT The bell rang too noisily.
[The adverb *noisily* modifies the action verb *rang*.]

Much confusion exists about the use of *good* and *well* in sentences. *Good* is an adjective. It cannot modify an action verb as an adverb does. For example, you should not say "She did it good." This should be "She did it well." The adverb *well* modifies the verb *did*.

EXAMPLES

RIGHT You threw a good pass. It looked good.

WRONG I think you pass good.

RIGHT I think you pass well.

EXERCISE 13 Number a sheet of paper 1–5. Next to each number write the word *good* or *well* that belongs in the sentence.

EXAMPLE He cooked a (good/well) stew.

good

1. The cake tasted (good/well) to me.
2. He made (good/well) frosting for it.
3. He spread it (good/well) all over the cake.
4. It made a (good/well) covering.
5. We all ate (good/well) that day.

The Double Negative

7m Avoid using a double negative.

Words that show a negative meaning are *no, not, none, never, nothing, no one, nobody,* and *hardly.* Sometimes you may want to use two negative words in a sentence. They may seem to make your point stronger. However, two negatives are not necessary. Be careful to use only one negative to show negative meaning.

EXAMPLES
RIGHT We never took any cookies.
WRONG We never took no cookies.

RIGHT We took no cookies.
RIGHT We took none.
WRONG We never took none.

EXERCISE 14 Number a sheet of paper 1–8. Rewrite correctly each sentence that has a double negative. Put *C* next to the number of each sentence that is correct.

EXAMPLE You cannot have none.

You cannot have any.

1. He never saw no wild animals.
2. He had no protective clothing.
3. No bugs never get to his skin.
4. He had no bites.
5. None of us was never so lucky.
6. At no time did any of us ever expect to get out alive.
7. We never found no reason to be sorry.
8. Our trip was not a success, though.

REVIEW EXERCISE A Agreement of Subject and Verb

Number a sheet of paper 1–15. Next to the number write the correct verb from the parentheses. Be sure that the verb agrees with its subject.

EXAMPLE Yoko (seem/seems) sad today.

seems

1. Kittens (are/is) furry, curious, and amusing.
2. They (are/is) also selfish and independent.
3. A kitten, or even a big cat, (need/needs) good care.
4. There (are/is) many books in the library about caring for a kitten.
5. Kittens, unlike an older cat, (eat/eats) several times each day.

6. Neither a kitten nor a cat (like/likes) very cold food.
7. About twenty degrees Celsius (is/are) the right temperature for a cat's food.
8. Calcium and bone meal (are/is) good for a kitten that does not like milk.
9. Good food and fresh water (is/are) good for a kitten's health.
10. Neither a kitten nor larger cats (is/are) happy with just food and water.
11. Toys and a place for play (make/makes) a kitten happy.
12. A toy that squeaks or crackles (is/are) fun for a kitten.
13. A ball tied to several bright colored strings (make/makes) a good toy.
14. If a dog or a young child (frighten/frightens) a new kitten, the kitten must be helped.
15. Of all the rules about caring for a kitten, the most important one (is/are) to be sure to talk to it.

REVIEW EXERCISE B More Subject-Verb Agreement

Number a sheet of paper 1–15. If the subject and verb of the following sentences agree, write *C* (correct) on your paper. If the subject and verb do not agree, write the correct verb form on your paper.

EXAMPLES John and Susan are navigators.

Susan, with several friends, have sailed across the river.

has sailed

1. Neither Lynda nor two of her three brothers like to camp.
2. Only Patricia, with some friends from school, camps in the mountains.
3. One problem on camping trips is mosquitoes.
4. One of these insects bite Patricia every year when she goes to the mountains.
5. A swarm of mosquitoes sometimes land on her face.
6. Patricia also gets blisters from hiking in the mountains.
7. A box of bandages is an important part of Patricia's camping equipment.
8. The beauty of the mountains makes the trip pleasant for her.
9. Fishing, as well as hiking, climbing, and swimming, are a part of the fun.
10. Neither Patricia nor her friends fish very well.
11. One of the friends has never caught a fish.
12. Either she or her friend fall asleep sitting by the river.
13. A whole school of fish swims peacefully by while Patricia sleeps.
14. Even if ants eat her lunch and mosquitoes eat her, Patricia enjoys camping.
15. The two weeks in the mountains are the best weeks of Patricia's summer.

REVIEW EXERCISE C Verbs

Number a sheet of paper 1–10. Next to each number, write the correct verb form from within the parentheses.

1. Rolanda has (rode/ridden) a bicycle for many years.
2. She has also (drove/driven) a motor bike.
3. Now she has (began/begun) to learn to ride a unicycle.
4. Last week she went shopping and (chose/chosen) a red unicycle.
5. She first (saw/seen) it pictured in a magazine.
6. Jenny has (taken/took) some unicycle riding lessons, too.
7. She even (done/did) some tricks on her cycle for a school play.
8. She rode backwards and (rang/rung) the cycle's noisy bell.
9. A reporter has (written/wrote) an article about Jenny for the school newspaper.
10. Jenny and Rolanda have (gone/went) to the library to find out who invented the unicycle.

REVIEW EXERCISE D Correct Pronouns

Number a sheet of paper 1–15. Next to each number, write the correct form of the pronoun in parentheses.

EXAMPLE The coach gave instructions to (we/us) swimmers.

1. My family and (I/me) visited Washington, D.C.
2. On holidays they and (I/me) like to visit historic places.
3. (We/Us) travelers wanted to see the White House, the Capitol Building, and Arlington National Cemetery.
4. A guide first took (us/we) to the White House.
5. The guide told my brother and (I/me) that the president was in the White House that day.
6. He said that my brother and (I/me) should watch carefully; we might see the president.
7. My sister was also with (us/we).
8. Her friend and (she/her) had written to the president.
9. When my sister saw a man getting into an elevator, she shouted to (he/him).
10. Her shouts embarrassed my brother and (I/me).
11. He and (I/me) walked away from our sister.
12. He and (I/me) got to see the ballroom where Mrs. John Adams once hung her laundry.
13. (We/Us) boys saw the picture of George Washington and remembered the story of Dolly Madison.
14. (She/Her) saved the picture when the British burned the White House in 1814.
15. Many Americans still give thanks to (she/her) for saving that famous picture.

REVIEW EXERCISE E Adverbs and Adjectives

Number a sheet of paper 1–10. Next to the number, write the correct word from the parentheses. You will be choosing between an adverb and an adjective.

1. Felicita has trained her twelve-year-old dog Lucy very (well/good).
2. The dog rolls over on command and sits up (nice/nicely).
3. She gives a (quiet/quietly) bark when she is asked to speak.
4. She goes (quick/quickly) when Felicita asks her to fetch a newspaper.
5. She has been trained so (well/good) that Felicita entered her in a dog show.
6. At the show, Lucy behaved (bad/badly).
7. She is always a (good/well) dog, but she was afraid of the judges at the show.
8. When they asked her to roll over, she barked (noisy/noisily).
9. She sat up (good/well) but not when she was told to.
10. Lucy learns (quick/quickly), but she hates dog shows.

REVIEW EXERCISE F **Vocabulary**

Review the following words.

anxious, conscious, earnest, immature, natural, ridiculous

Number a sheet of paper 1–5. Write each sentence with a blank, filling in the blank with the adverb form of the underlined word.

EXAMPLE Mr. Wong was anxious to get his tax bill.
Mr. Wong waited ____________ for his tax bill.

anxiously

1. It was immature of Doreen to cry when she scratched her knee.
   Doreen sometimes behaves ____________.
2. Grapes are a delicious natural snack.
   Grapes grow ____________ in vineyards.
3. The student was earnest in her efforts to succeed in the assignment.
   "Write this word first," the teacher said ____________.
4. A heavy winter coat looks ridiculous on a hot summer day.
   "That coat looks ____________ heavy for this summer day," said Arisba.
5. The bus driver was irritable by the end of the day.
   "Why didn't you walk home?" he asked me ____________.

CHAPTER

8

COMMON CONFUSIONS

Do you ever wonder which word to use in a sentence? Maybe you have forgotten the exact meaning of a term. This chapter will help you answer questions about words and their forms that are easily confused.

The words are listed in alphabetical order so that you can quickly find what you need. If you want to know how to spell and use *all right,* look under the *A's* on page 173. The difference between *your* and *you're* is found under the *Y's* on page 189. With almost every term there are examples and a short practice exercise.

ALPHABETICAL LISTING

A/an: Use the article *an* before words that start with the sounds these letters stand for: **a, e, i, o,** and **u.**

EXAMPLES *an ant, ape, aviator*
an eatery, empty lot, elevator
an injury, insider, imp
an open window, otter, oven, honor
an undertaker, upset (Note: when the letter **u** "says its own name," use only *a,* as in *a unicorn, a unit.*)

Use the article *a* before words beginning with the sounds of *all* other letters:

EXAMPLES *a bean, king, monster, runner, trotter, whip, van.*

Notice that no **x** word is given. Almost all words that begin with **x** are said with **z** sounds, for example, *xylophone. X-ray* begins with an **e** sound, like that in *extra.*

Accept/except: *Accept* means "to agree to receive something."

EXAMPLES It is hard to *accept* criticism.
It is easy to *accept* praise.

Except means "leaving out" or "other than."

EXAMPLES Everybody *except* Marvin may leave.
Give me anything *except* uncooked fish.

EXERCISE 1 Write the following sentences on a sheet of paper. Fill in each blank with *accept* or *except.*

1. Would you ____________ this present?
2. I like most people ____________ complainers.

3. How could you ____________ his offer?
4. We can have everyone ____________ Bill to the party.

Advice/advise: *Advice* is a noun that means "an opinion, information, or suggestion that someone gives."

EXAMPLES Her *advice* was to stay out of fights.
That sounds like good *advice* to me.

Advise is a verb that means "to give an opinion, information, or suggestion."

EXAMPLES I *advise* you not to get into a fight.
She *advises* everyone to talk things out.

EXERCISE 2 Write the following sentences on a sheet of paper. Fill in each blank with *advice* or *advise.*

1. My mom offers good ____________.
2. I ____________ you to take the bus.
3. Everybody gives ____________, but few take it.
4. Let me ____________ you to straighten that out.

Am not, are not, is not/ain't: *Ain't* is a word that some people use in speaking to stand for *am not, are not,* or *is not. Ain't* is not generally accepted for formal usage.

WRITE I *am not* chewing loudly.
not
I *ain't* chewing loudly.

WRITE He *isn't* doing anything.
not
He *ain't* doing anything.

WRITE We *aren't* going.
not
We *ain't* going.

When you write, use *am not, aren't,* or *isn't* instead of *ain't*.

EXERCISE 3 Write the following sentences on a sheet of paper. Use *am not, aren't,* or *isn't* in place of *ain't*.

1. I ain't going to do it.
2. That gun ain't at my house.
3. The police ain't here yet.
4. I ain't asking again!

All right/alright: *All right* is correctly written as two words. *Alright* is not a word in English.

Almost/most: *Almost* means "very nearly; all but."

EXAMPLES She is *almost* fifteen.
Almost everybody in my class is older.

Most can mean "more than anything else."

EXAMPLES It was the *most* horrible movie I ever saw.
She was the *most* excited person I've ever seen.

Most can also mean "the greatest amount."

EXAMPLES She had *most* of the junk hidden somewhere.
We have come *most* of the way.

Sometimes *most* can mean "almost all."

EXAMPLE I like *most* vegetables.

Most should not be used as a short form of *almost.*

WRITE She is *almost* done.
not
She is *most* done.

WRITE She ate *almost* all the cookies.
not
She ate *most* all the cookies.

EXERCISE 4 Copy the following sentences on a sheet of paper. Replace *most* with *almost* whenever it belongs. Some sentences do not need correcting.

1. Most everything was lost in the flood.
2. Most of the time she dreams of going back.
3. Bessie dislikes most movies.
4. She ate most all the popcorn.

Already/all ready: *Already* means "before now."

EXAMPLES I *already* know how to read.
I learned that *already.*

The words *all* and *ready* are two different words which mean "all of something is ready."

EXAMPLES They are *all ready* to learn how to drive.
Is everyone *all ready* to go?

Do not confuse the one word *already* with the two words *all* and *ready.*

WRITE Most of us are *all ready* to leave.
not
Most of us are *already* to leave.

WRITE Are we *all ready?*
not
Are we *already?*

EXERCISE 5 Copy the following sentences on a sheet of paper. Fill in each blank with *already* or *all ready.*

1. We are here ____________.
2. The doughnuts are ____________ to go.
3. They have ____________ been eaten.
4. We were ____________ to eat them.
5. I have ____________ started cooking another batch.

Among/between: The meaning of these two words is very similar. *Among* means "together with others" or "in the company of others." *Among* is used when you are talking about more than two things.

EXAMPLES He is *among* his friends.
They say there is no honor *among* thieves.

Between means "something shared by two people or things."

EXAMPLES *Between* us, Peggy and I have $25.00.
Just *between* you and me, I don't believe it.

Use *among* when you are talking about three or more. Use *between* when you are talking about only two.

WRITE There's not a loser *among* the four of us.
not
There's not a loser *between* the four of us.

WRITE What's a dollar *among* three friends?
not
What's a dollar *between* three friends?

EXERCISE 6 Write the following sentences on a sheet of paper. Fill in each blank with *among* or *between.*

1. No one __________ us five has any money.
2. He and we argue who __________ us should pay.
3. The cost is __________ two and three dollars.
4. Split up the cost __________ all of us.

Bring/take: *Bring* means "to carry something nearer."

EXAMPLE *Bring* the pie to me.

Take means "to carry something away."

EXAMPLE *Take* the empty pan with you.

Cannot/can not: Both ways of writing the word are correct. They both mean "not able to." *Can not* gives more emphasis to a statement.

EXAMPLE She *cannot* be here. She *can not* be here.

Can/may: *Can* means "to know how to do something" or "to be able to do something."

EXAMPLES I *can* dribble a basketball well.
I *can* dance all right if I want to.

May means "something is possible or likely" or "someone is to be allowed to do something."

EXAMPLES She says she *may* come if she has time.
May I go?

To be correct, use *may* when you mean "to ask or give permission."

WRITE *May* I have it?
not
Can I have it?

WRITE You *may* go now.
not
You *can* go now.

EXERCISE 7 Write the following sentences on a sheet of paper. Put *may* or *can* in each blank.

1. We ______ reach the top by noon if we hurry.
2. Yes, you ______ stay out late.
3. ______ you repair the faucet?
4. ______ I visit you at your house?

Can hardly/can't hardly: *Hardly* means "barely." *Can hardly* means "can barely."

EXAMPLES He *can hardly* do it.
[It's hard. He can barely do it.]

I *can hardly* reach it.
[I can just barely reach it.]

Always write *can hardly,* never *can't hardly.*

WRITE I *can hardly* see.
not
I *can't hardly* see.

WRITE I *can hardly* understand.
not
I *can't hardly* understand.

Could have/could of: *Could of* does not make sense. People write it by mistake. When they say *could have* quickly, it usually sounds like *could've*. *Could've* sounds like *could of* to many people and so they may write it down wrong.

WRITE I *could have* done it.
not
I *could of* done it.

WRITE She *could have* been a champion runner.
not
She *could of* been a champion runner.

Good/well: *Good* means "better than usual or average."

EXAMPLES This is really *good* ice cream.
He did a *good* job.

Well means "in a way that is good or pleasing."

EXAMPLES She did it *well*.
He really draws *well*.

Good is an adjective, a word that describes a noun.

EXAMPLES She's a *good* friend.
That's a *good* place.

Well is usually an adverb, a word that describes a verb.

EXAMPLES She runs *well*.
That works *well*.

WRITE He sings *well.*
not
He sings *good.*

WRITE She did the job *well.*
not
She did the job *good.*

EXERCISE 8 Write the following sentences on a sheet of paper. Fill in the blanks with *good* or *well.*

1. She sang ______.
2. Hers was a ______ job.
3. Carlos was a ______ two hours early.
4. He spent the time ______.

I/me: *I* means "the person speaking or writing."

EXAMPLES *I* am very thirsty.
I like salmon.

Me means "the person who receives the action" or "the person something is done to."

EXAMPLES She likes *me.*
The donkey bit *me.*

WRITE Andy and *I* went downtown.
not
Andy and *me* went downtown.

WRITE Beth and *I* will go.
not
Beth and *me* will go.

EXERCISE 9 Write the following sentences on a sheet of paper. Fill in each blank with *I* or *me.*

1. I chased the elephant. The elephant chased ______.
2. Beth knows Suzie. ______ know Beth but not Suzie.
3. Candice punched ______ on my nose.
4. ______ left Candice alone.

Its/it's: *Its* is a possessive word. The **s** on the end either means "ownership, owning something," or it means that "the thing that follows is a part of it."

EXAMPLES I like the sweater because of *its* color.
[Color is part of it.]

Do you like *its* looks?
[Looks are a part of it.]

It's means the same thing as *it is.* The apostrophe (') stands for the missing letter **i** in the word *is.*

EXAMPLES *It's* not fun to play with someone who cheats.
It's better now.

EXERCISE 10 Write the following sentences on a sheet of paper. Correct any mistakes in the use of *its* or *it's.*

1. Did you notice it's ears?
2. Its missing a tail.
3. It's hair is dirty.
4. Can we fix it's left front paw?
5. Its no use. We might as well throw it away.

Lead/led: When both these words are pronounced the same, they are called *homonyms.* When they are homonyms, *l-e-a-d* is a word that names a metal.

EXAMPLE They mined *lead.*

L-e-d, which is said the same way, describes an action that happened in the past.

EXAMPLE Long ago Harriet Tubman *led* the slaves to safety.

EXERCISE 11 Write the following sentences on a sheet of paper. Fill in the blanks with *led* or *lead.*

1. The mine ran out of ______.
2. Last year the scout ______ the party through the pass.
3. She ______ them home yesterday.
4. The bullet was made of ______.

Learn/teach: *Learn* and *teach* have different meanings. Someone *teaches* something *to* someone. Someone *learns* something *from* someone.

Remember: A *learner* or student *learns from* a teacher. A *teacher teaches* something *to* a learner.

Lie/lay: *Lie* means "to stretch out one's body" or "to tell an untruth." However, *lie* in the first meaning is an irregular verb. *Lie* in the second meaning is a regular verb and forms its past tense by adding **d.**

Lie (irregular verb) "to stretch out one's body."

PRESENT	PAST	PRESENT PERFECT
lie	lay	have lain

EXAMPLES Our dog *lies* near the stove at night.
He *lay* there all day yesterday.
He *has lain* in that spot for hours.

Lie (regular verb) "to tell an untruth."

PRESENT	PAST	PRESENT PERFECT
lie	lied	have lied

EXAMPLES Would the witness *lie* to the jury?
She *lied* about the illness.
He *has lied* before.

Lay means "to put something down." In this meaning it always takes an object.

PRESENT	PAST	PRESENT PERFECT
lay	laid	have laid

EXAMPLES Should we *lay* the foundation for this building?
They *laid* another foundation yesterday.
The workmen *have laid* many good foundations.

EXERCISE 12 Write the following sentences on your paper. Fill in each blank with the correct form of the verb in parentheses.

1. A person who has _____ all his life has difficulty not lying anymore. (lie—"to tell an untruth")
2. Yesterday the builders _____ several rows of bricks. (lay—"to put something down")
3. She _____ on the couch while her mother read a story. (lie—"to stretch out one's body")

4. The lot was ______ out to allow the foundation to be built here. (lay—"to put something down")
5. The cat ______ on the waterbed when no one is home. (lie—"to stretch out one's body")

OK, O.K., okay/all right: All of the three spellings of *okay* are common. In writing, it is usually better to use *all right* instead of *okay.*

Rise/raise: *Rise* means "to get up." It is an irregular verb.

PRESENT	PAST	PRESENT PERFECT
rise	rose	have risen

EXAMPLES The scouts *rise* early and leave the camp before sunrise.
When the sun *rose,* the camp was nearly empty.
After the biscuit dough *has risen,* put it into the tin.

Raise means "to lift up." *Raise* is a regular verb and always takes an object.

PRESENT	PAST	PRESENT PERFECT
raise	raised	have raised

EXAMPLES *Raise* the tent poles.
The campers *raised* the tents.
Since prehistoric times, parents *have raised* their children.

Set/sit: These two words are often confused. *Set* is the word you use when you put something in a certain way or place:

EXAMPLES He *set* the knife down.
She *set* the table.

Sit is the word you use when telling about an action that changes the position of a person or an animal.

EXAMPLES Teachers always make children *sit* down.
The lion *sits* quietly.

WRITE I will *set* it down.
not
I will *sit* it down.

WRITE Please *sit* down.
not
Please *set* down.

EXERCISE 13 Write the following sentences on a sheet of paper. Fill in the blanks with *set* or *sit*.

1. Tiny, you should ______ beside Arlis.
2. You can ______ the books on the other side.
3. Then you and she will have room to ______ together.
4. There will be time after you ______ the table.

Should of/should have: *Should of* does not make sense. People write it by mistake. When they say *should have* quickly, it usually sounds like *should've. Should've* sounds like *should of* to many people, and so they write it down wrong.

WRITE I *should have* done it.
not
I *should of* done it.

WRITE She *should have* been a great player.
not
She *should of* been a great player.

Them (there)/those: *Them* and *them there* should not be written instead of *those*.

WRITE *Those* books . . . *Those* people . . .
not
Them books . . . *Them there* people . . .

EXERCISE 14 Write the following sentences on a sheet of paper. Use *those* instead of *them* and *them there.*

1. A few of them there dresses look good.
2. I think them salespeople are rude.
3. They should take a lesson from them there people who teach manners.
4. Them people could learn a thing or two.

Their/there/they're: These three words are often said the same way. They are *homonyms. Their* is a word that shows ownership. It is the possessive form of the pronoun *they.*

EXAMPLES Sarah is *their* chimpanzee.
We are going to *their* house.

There tells where something happens. It is an adverb.

EXAMPLES I saw them *there.*
I met her *there.*

They're means *they + are.*

EXAMPLES *They're* here now.
They're the ones I mean.

Because these three words sound alike, they may cause spelling errors.

EXERCISE 15 Write the following sentences on a sheet of paper. Correct every spelling error in the use of *their, there,* or *they're.*

1. Their looking at there roof over they're.
2. Their are no frogs in they're pond.
3. They're water has run out of their.
4. Their is the place to find their hose.
5. They're, now you've ruined there plans.

These, this, that/these here, this here, that here: *These* and *this* mean something close; they do not need the extra word *here* to make their meaning clear.

That means something farther away; it does not need the extra word *there* to make its meaning clear.

WRITE *These* things are hard.
not
These here things are hard.
WRITE *That* book is closed.
not
That there book is closed.

EXERCISE 16 Write the following sentences on a sheet of paper. Correct them by taking out *here* and *there* when they are not needed.

1. That there dog is a mean hound.
2. This here cat was bitten by it.
3. The cat jumped up on this here ledge.
4. He knocked that there flower pot off.
5. It hit that there dog on the tail.

To/too/two: These three words are *homonyms*. The word *to* usually introduces another word or group of words.

EXAMPLES *To* him, *to* the lake, *to* be pleased.

Too means "also."

EXAMPLES I want some, *too*. I can do it, *too*.

Two is a number meaning "one more than one."

EXAMPLES He had *two* pet snails. I had *two*, too.

Because all three words are said alike, they may cause spelling problems.

EXERCISE 17 Write the following sentences on a sheet of paper. Correct every spelling error in the use of *to, too,* or *two*.

1. Too toots on the horn make to much noise.
2. The music is two bad too listen too, two.
3. In to hours I may be two tired too care.

Try and/try to: Usually you should write *try to* instead of *try and*. Someone tries *to* do something.

WRITE *Try to* come.
not
Try and come.

WRITE I'll *try to* see if I can.
not
I'll *try and* see if I can.

EXERCISE 18 Write the following sentences on a sheet of paper. Correct every sentence.

1. Try and eat your breakfast.
2. I try and keep you well fed.
3. But you don't try and stay healthy.
4. Let's try and get you fatter.

We/us: Some people make the mistake of saying "Us people . . ." in a sentence such as, "We people know what's good for us." The pronoun *us* should not be used as part of the subject of a verb.

WRITE *We* players should practice in the gym.
not
Us players should practice in the gym.

Who/whom: *Who* and *whom* are different forms of the same word. In most cases when someone is speaking, *who* is used.

EXAMPLES *Who* tried the hardest?
Who wants some gum?
Who do you mean?
Who am I talking to?

Who should not be used after a word like *to, from,* or *for.*

WRITE *To whom, for whom, from whom*
not
to who, for who, from who

Whose/who's: These two words are *homonyms.* *Whose* is a form of *who* that shows ownership or possession.

EXAMPLES *Whose* house did you go to?
[Who owns the house?]

I know *whose* mitt that is.
[I know who the mitt belongs to.]

Who's is a form of *who* and *is.* The apostrophe (') takes the place of the **i** in the word *is* or the letters **ha** in the word *has.*

EXAMPLES She's always the one *who's* right.
Who's got the nerve to try it?
Who's been here before?

Remember: Use *who's* only when you mean *who is* or *who has*.

EXERCISE 19 Rewrite each following sentence that has a *whose/who's* error in it. Correct the error.

1. Whose foolish enough to jump from here?
2. Who's glider can you use?
3. Who's going to try it first?
4. Whose left who's legs are strong?

Your/you're: These two words are *homonyms*. *Your* is the possessive form of *you*. It shows ownership.

EXAMPLES It's *your* day to do whatever you want.
Let's go to *your* place.

You're means *you* + *are*.

EXAMPLES *You're* right.
I think *you're* mean!

EXERCISE 20 Rewrite each sentence that has a *your/you're* error in it. Correct the error.

1. Your the first one here.
2. Did you bring you're lunch?
3. Your not seriously thinking of skipping lunch?
4. Your going to reduce you're waistline.

REVIEW EXERCISE A Homonyms

Number a sheet of paper 1–10. If the underlined word is used correctly, write *C* (correct) on your paper. If the underlined word is used incorrectly, rewrite it correctly.

EXAMPLE Who's tomb are we visiting?
Whose

1. If you're going to do homework, have everything ready for work.
2. Its a good idea to have a snack before sitting down to work.
3. You cannot work well if your hungry.
4. If you eat to much, you will fall asleep.
5. Whose room should you study in?
6. A student who's house is too noisy may want to study in a public library.
7. Its always quiet there.
8. The noise in her house led one student to get up early in the morning to study.
9. You're going to need at least two lead pencils, a good eraser, and a good light.
10. With all these tools, you're sure to learn about homonyms and their use.

REVIEW EXERCISE B Usage

Number a sheet of paper 1–15. Next to each number write the correct word in parentheses.

1. What would you do if you found a $100 bill (lying/laying) on a sidewalk?

2. With all of that money a person (can/may) buy many things.
3. You could share the money (between/among) you and one good friend.
4. The friend with (who/whom) you shared might want to buy some ice skates, a bicycle, or some fancy shoes.
5. He or she might just want to (sit/set) in front of the $100 bill and look at it.
6. Having that much money might (learn/teach) you to spend carefully.
7. A rich person sometimes (accepts/excepts) advice from a banker.
8. You might begin to wonder (whose/who's) money you had found.
9. Your own conscience might (advise/advice) you to look for the owner.
10. No one would just (lay/lie) a large amount of money down on the street.
11. Some person (could have/could of) dropped the money accidentally.
12. He (should have/should of) come back to look for it.
13. He may not have looked (good/well) enough to find his money.
14. To (who/whom) should you report that you have found the money?
15. You will feel (good/well) when you have returned the money to its true owner.

REVIEW EXERCISE C **Usage**

Number a sheet of paper 1–10. If the underlined word is correctly used, write *C* (correct) after the number. If the underlined word is incorrectly used, write the correct word after the number.

EXAMPLE A African buffalo may weigh as much as seven hundred kilograms.

1. The leopard is stealthy when it hunts it's prey.
2. Two leopards may hunt together and share the meat between them.
3. Because the leopard is aggressive, it hunts good.
4. Leopard cubs play and lie in the sunshine, but adult leopards sleep by day and hunt by night.
5. When the moon rises, the leopards are hunting in Africa.
6. A leopard is fierce with its enemies and gentle with it's cubs.
7. The older animals learn the cubs to protect themselves.
8. Even the young cub is all ready an excellent hunter.
9. Among them, the two leopard parents teach the cubs to survive.
10. From whom have we learned most about leopards?

REVIEW EXERCISE D Usage

Number a sheet of paper 1–10. On your paper write the word that comes before the error, the word in error, and the word after each error in the following paragraphs. Correct each of the errors.

One morning my sister and me looked out our window and saw an unicorn lying on the hood of our uncle's car. Perhaps we should have gone back to sleep or at least have kept the unicorn a secret among the two of us. Instead, we couldn't hardly wait to get dressed and run down to see that unicorn.

We girls had read about unicorns. Unicorns are beautiful, but they're not real. Their imaginary beasts. Can ordinary girls see imaginary beasts on their uncle's car, I wondered.

While I was wondering, my sister was already talking to the unicorn. It woke up slowly and rose its lovely head. My sister thought that she must try and be polite. She set down on the curb and said, "Ain't you hungry?"

The unicorn, whom I already liked, turned it's soft brown eyes and its golden horn toward my sister. "We imaginary animals do not have to eat," it said. "We need love, but we do not need food." It lay its head gently on my sister's lap. Later it walked down the street and around the corner by the gas station.

Our uncle now parks his car in a garage.

REVIEW EXERCISE E **Vocabulary**

Review the following words.

ADJECTIVES	NOUNS
aggressive	aviator
brutal	buffalo
desperate	ghost
fierce	leopard
stealthy	seafarer

Now combine one adjective with one noun and any necessary articles to form a title. Finally, write a paragraph on the subject named in the title. Avoid usage errors in your paragraph.

EXAMPLE An Aggressive Buffalo

UNIT FOUR

MECHANICS

Capitalization
Punctuation

CHAPTER

9

CAPITALIZATION

Capital letters are used in writing to call attention to words. You probably know many of the rules for capitalizing. For example, there is the rule to capitalize the first word in a sentence. Some other rules may not be so familiar to you. This chapter will give you guidelines for using capital letters.

CAPITAL LETTERS

9a Capitalize the first word in a sentence.

Always begin the first word of a sentence with a capital letter.

EXAMPLES The room had only a bare table in its center.
Into the room marched Wanda.

9b Capitalize the pronoun *I*.

EXAMPLE When will **I** find them?

Note: Do not capitalize *my* or any other pronoun unless it begins a sentence.

9c Capitalize proper nouns.

Proper nouns are names of particular persons, places, or things. They should always begin with capital letters. See Nouns, pp. 5–6

EXAMPLES **O**liver **P**erry (but not *man*)
Annie **O**akley (but not *woman*)
Cincinnati (but not *city*)
Time (but not *magazine*)

(1) Capitalize the names of particular people and animals.

EXAMPLES Is that you, **R**everend **J**essup?
Have you seen our cat, **S**napper?

(2) Capitalize the names of particular places.

EXAMPLES

Cities, Towns	**S**t. **L**ouis, **H**ouston, **A**rdmore
States, Counties	**M**ississippi, **O**range **C**ounty
Countries	**M**exico, **C**anada
Continents	**A**sia, **A**ustralia
Special regions	the **S**outh, **N**ew **E**ngland, the **N**orthwest

Bodies of water, Islands, Points of land	the **C**aribbean **S**ea, the **G**ulf of **M**exico, **L**ong **I**sland, **P**oint **R**eyes
Parks	**C**utter **P**ark, the **E**verglades
Roadways	**S**tate **S**treet, **I**nter-state 80

Note: Do not capitalize directions.

EXAMPLE "Go east, young woman" is the latest bit of advice.

EXERCISE 1 Number a sheet of paper 1–10. Next to each number, write the words that need capital letters. Add capitals where they belong.

EXAMPLE We saw the statue of abraham lincoln in washington.

Abraham Lincoln, Washington

1. the colorado river runs through colorado and arizona.
2. two men, bradley and powell, shot the colorado rapids near the turn of the century.
3. powell had lost his arm in the civil war.
4. he came to the southwest to explore the grand canyon.
5. it was while reading about powell that i became interested in evel knievel.
6. rather than shooting the rapids, knievel tried to jump the snake river.
7. he had already jumped his motorcycle in europe and all over america.

8. i saw him jump his bike over a row of buses in london.
9. after his last jump, evel said that he had not had enough.
10. i wonder what mr. powell would think of evel knievel.

(3) Capitalize important words in the names of organizations, institutions, businesses, and branches of government.

When only initials are written, capitalize them. Usually omit periods.

EXAMPLES

Organizations	**N**ational **C**ollegiate **A**thletic **A**ssociation (**NCAA**), the **M**arine **C**orps
Institutions	**U**niversity of **P**ennsylvania, **P**lains **J**unior **H**igh
Businesses and their products	**G**eneral **M**otors, **T**hunderbird, **P**roctor and **G**amble, **C**heer
Branches of government	the **S**enate, the **S**tate **D**epartment

(4) Capitalize school subjects when they are used as names of particular courses.

EXAMPLES Some of us signed up for **W**oodworking I.
We learned a lot about woodworking.

We learned more government last year in **C**ivics II.

(5) Capitalize the names of nationalities, races, and religions.

EXAMPLES **I**ndians, **A**rabians, **S**paniards, **B**aptists

(6) Capitalize the name of God and other beings worshipped by people.

EXAMPLES **J**ehovah, the **A**lmighty, **Z**eus, **B**uddha, **G**od

EXERCISE 2 Number a sheet of paper 1–12. Next to each number, write the words that need capital letters. Add capitals where they belong.

EXAMPLE In general science we studied an almost extinct species of salamander that lives in nigeria.

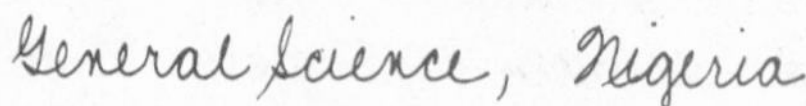

1. In recent years, the united states air force has been doing a study on unidentified flying objects.
2. Even congress said that studies should be done.
3. Recently, a show on nbc television described the air force study.
4. Many people wrote to the institute of outer space to tell of their experiences.
5. One college even gave a course called preparing for alien visitors.

6. People say they have actually seen strange objects shaped a little like volkswagens but traveling much faster.
7. Other people claim there is a landing strip high in the peruvian andes where flying objects land.
8. Even universities, such as the university of southern california, are interested in them.
9. Some people hope that beings from another planet will unite americans, chinese, and russians.
10. It would be helpful if someone from outer space could stop the quarreling that goes on in the currie park playground.
11. How would it be to have a martian in the united nations?
12. In the meantime, the sigs toy company has made toy flying objects.

(7) Capitalize important words in the names of historical events, periods, or other special events.

EXAMPLES **L**abor **D**ay, the **W**ar **B**etween the **S**tates, **F**ather's **D**ay, the **M**iddle **A**ges, **O**ctober

Note: Do not capitalize seasons of the year (fall, summer).

(8) Capitalize the first word and every important word in the titles of people, books, magazines, newspapers, movies, television shows, and other works people produce.

EXAMPLES

People	**C**ongressman **J**ones, **S**ergeant **S**carpino, **A**unt **R**uth (but not any aunt)
Books, Stories	***O**ld **T**estament, **T**he **R**ed **P**ony,* "**T**he **F**all of the **H**ouse of **U**sher"
Poems	"**S**topping by **W**oods on a **S**nowy **E**vening"
Magazines	***N**ational **G**eographic, **T**ime*
Newspapers	the ***P**ost-**D**ispatch,* the ***D**aily **N**ews*
Movies, TV shows	***T**he **G**reat **T**rain **R**obbery,*
Works of music, architecture, art	"**P**ick a **N**umber" *Carmen,* the **E**iffel **T**ower

EXERCISE 3 Copy the following sentences on a sheet of paper. Put in capital letters where they belong.

1. The *national geographic* had an article about Greece by melville grosvernor.
2. The people of ancient Greece worshipped the sea-god poseidon.
3. The ruins of the temple of poseidon still stand above the sea.
4. The temple stands as a reminder of the period in Greece's history called the golden age.
5. While reading the article, I was reminded of the movie *ulysses*.

9d Capitalize proper adjectives.

EXAMPLES a **C**hinese vase, an **I**daho potato, **G**reek myths, **J**ewish holidays

9e Capitalize the first word of a sentence in a direct quotation.

EXAMPLES Tillie asked, "**W**hich way do I go to reach Camden?"
Marie answered, "**I**t's about five miles straight ahead."

EXERCISE 4 Number a sheet of paper 1–5. Next to each number, write the word that should be capitalized. Add capitals where they belong.

EXAMPLE Tim thought to himself, "a sandwich would taste good."

a

1. Tim called out, "where's the jam?"
2. A voice answered, "look on the bottom shelf."
3. Tim looked and saw nothing, so he said, "it's not there."
4. He continued, "did you take it?"
5. The voice answered again, "if you look in the cupboard and not the refrigerator, you'll find it."

REVIEW EXERCISE A Capitalization

Number a sheet of paper 1–10. Next to each number, write the words that need capitals. Capitalize those words.

EXAMPLE i like to take trips to different parts of the united states.

I, United States

1. last month, I visited my grandparents in bloomington, indiana.
2. my grandfather recently retired from working in a general motors plant in detroit.
3. he has a grant from the ford foundation to write a book on the automobile industry.
4. he has visited the ford factory, the volkswagen plant, and his old employer, gm.
5. the last book he wrote was reviewed in *time* and *newsweek*.
6. it was about the effects of industry on the wildlife of the southwest.
7. my grandfather said, "writing these books keeps me young."
8. he's also very concerned with the wildlife in lake erie.
9. he told me, "making cars shouldn't kill fish."
10. when i returned to new york, i had a lot to think about.

REVIEW EXERCISE B Capitalization

Number a sheet of paper 1–25. In each of the following pairs of sentences, one sentence is correctly capitalized and the other is incorrectly capitalized. Next to each number on your paper write the letter of the correct sentence.

EXAMPLE A. Felicita went to atlanta on monday.
B. Felicita went to Atlanta on Monday.

B

1. A. I am taking Spanish and math.
   B. I am taking Spanish and Math.
2. A. One of the Greek gods was Apollo.
   B. One of the Greek Gods was Apollo.
3. A. My class saw *Romeo and Juliet* at the Curan Theater.
   B. My class saw *Romeo and Juliet* at the curan theater.
4. A. Dr. Gum is a well-known Orthodontist.
   B. Dr. Gum is a well-known orthodontist.
5. A. We will meet at the corner of Church street and Sanchez avenue.
   B. We will meet at the corner of Church Street and Sanchez Avenue.
6. A. My uncle works at the Ford Motor Company.
   B. My uncle works at the Ford Motor company.
7. A. Brandeis is a University in Waltham, Massachusetts.
   B. Brandeis is a university in Waltham, Massachusetts.
8. A. The Pacific Gas and Electric Company supplies power to parts of California.
   B. The Pacific gas and electric company supplies power to parts of California.
9. A. Ancient Greeks worshipped many gods.
   B. Ancient Greeks worshipped many Gods.

10. A. Hiroshi's father works in the Goodman building.
    B. Hiroshi's father works in the Goodman Building.
11. A. The people of Ethiopia fear a Civil War.
    B. The people of Ethiopia fear a civil war.
12. A. Next Fall Ellen will take a course in Geometry.
    B. Next fall Ellen will take a course in geometry.
13. A. My neighbor is a senior in high school.
    B. My neighbor is a senior in High School.
14. A. Huckleberry Finn found a raft on the Mississippi River.
    B. Huckleberry Finn found a raft on the Mississippi river.
15. A. I wrote a letter to Mr. Gradgrind, Superintendent of Schools.
    B. I wrote a letter to Mr. Gradgrind, superintendent of schools.
16. A. Charleston is a large city named for an English king.
    B. Charleston is a large City named for an English king.
17. A. The dry weather seems to be moving West.
    B. The dry weather seems to be moving west.
18. A. There have been two Governor Browns in California.
    B. There have been two governor Browns in California.
19. A. Agnes enjoys bocks about the West.
    B. Agnes enjoys books about the west.
20. A. Giannini Junior High School is the largest junior high school in Oregon.

B. Giannini Junior High School is the largest Junior High School in Oregon.

21. A. Zoomer wants to be your Automobile Company.

 B. Zoomer wants to be your automobile company.

22. A. Theodore Roosevelt fought in the Spanish American War.

 B. Theodore Roosevelt fought in the Spanish American war.

23. A. My Uncle Sergio has three uncles.

 B. My Uncle Sergio has three Uncles.

24. A. The Empire State building was once the tallest building in the world.

 B. The Empire State Building was once the tallest building in the world.

25. A. You may want to read an article in the *Daily News* about King Tutankhamen's tomb.

 B. You may want to read an article in the *Daily News* about king Tutankhamen's tomb.

REVIEW EXERCISE C **Capitalization**

Number a sheet of paper 1–19. You will find twenty errors in capitalization in the following paragraphs. Some words may need capitals. Other words should *not* have capitals. After each number write correctly the word that has an error in capitalization.

EXAMPLE 1. america

In the 1880's and 1890's children in rural america looked forward to the fourth-of-July celebration, the County fair in autumn, and the coming of the circus. The most famous of all American Circuses was operated by Phineas T. Barnum.

Mr. barnum, or professor Barnum as he liked to be called, was a good showman. When he started his circus in 1871, he called it "the Greatest show on Earth." Ten years later he joined J. A. Bailey to form the famous Barnum and Bailey Circus.

Every Spring the circus started its annual tour, traveling from town to town on dusty country roads. Agents traveled ahead of the show, putting up Advertisements on fence posts and in the windows of General stores.

Phineas Barnum once said, "the public likes to be humbugged." He was a king of humbug. His first success was with Joice Heth. She said that she was 161 years old. She also said that she had been a nurse to general George Washington when he was a little boy in 1740. Hundreds of people paid to see joice. Then Barnum admitted that she was a dummy made for him of Rubber and whalebone by the Jonas Toy company. The hundreds of people who had already seen her paid again to see how they had been cheated.

Barnum loved to advertise. Four days before he died, he asked the New York *Daily news* to print the news of his death. He enjoyed the excitement caused by the story. He was one of america's great Showmen.

CHAPTER

10

PUNCTUATION

End Punctuation, Commas

Nearly all *punctuation marks* in writing are used to show how the voice sounds in reading aloud. When you ask someone a question, for example, you ordinarily make the tone of your voice work in a special way. A question mark at the end of a written sentence shows that it should be spoken as a question.

Punctuation in writing also helps to show the meaning of a group of words. Read each of the following sentences.

1. They heard what Dave said.
2. They heard what Dave said?
3. "They heard what?" Dave said.

The period at the end of the first sentence shows it is a statement of fact. However, you do not know what Dave said. The second sentence is a question. The question mark at the end of it shows this. The third sentence tells exactly what Dave said. Quotation marks help make its meaning clear.

END PUNCTUATION

Every sentence ends with a mark of punctuation. There are three kinds of end marks: the *period,* the *question mark,* and the *exclamation mark.*

The Period

10a A period is used to mark the end of a statement or a request.

EXAMPLES The pages of the book are torn.
Please take care of this book.

10b A period is used after some abbreviations.

EXAMPLES Reef St. Dr.
Dec. A.D.

10c A period is usually used after an initial.

EXAMPLES Booker T. Washington is known throughout the world.
Send this package back to A. B. Smith

Certain sets of initials used often together do not use periods.

EXAMPLES UK (United Kingdom)
USA (United States of America)

OMB (Office of Management and Budget)

EXERCISE 1 Write out the following ten sentences. Put in periods where they are missing and circle them.

EXAMPLE The Civil War ended on Apr 9, 1865

The Civil War ended on Apr. 9, 1865.

1. Robert E Lee is thought by many to be one of our greatest generals
2. He was born in Stratford, Va, near Main St on Jan 19, 1807
3. He was nearly 6 ft tall and weighed 170 lb as a grown man
4. He graduated from the U S Military Academy with high honors in 1829 and first served at Ft Pulaski in Georgia
5. For three years he worked in Washington, D C, as an army engineer
6. Later he directed work in building the St Louis harbor
7. At the start of the Civil War, President Lincoln offered Gen Lee the field command of the U S Army
8. But Lee joined the Confederates and took command in 1862 after Gen J E Johnston was wounded
9. When the war ended, Gen Lee surrendered at Appomattox, Va, to Gen Ulysses S Grant
10. Lee died on Oct 12, 1870, and has become a hero throughout the USA

The Question Mark

See Sentence, p. 330

10d A question mark is used to mark the end of a sentence that asks a question.

EXAMPLES What time is it?
Has Dracula come out of his coffin?

EXERCISE 2 Copy the following sentences on a separate sheet of paper. End punctuation has been omitted. Put a period after each statement or request. Put a question mark after each question.

1. Open the lid
2. What do you see inside
3. Can you see his fangs
4. He should be waking up any minute
5. Get the stake ready
6. Why are you frightened
7. He cannot hurt you now
8. Is this the wrong man

The Exclamation Mark

10e An exclamation mark is used at the end of a strong statement.

An exclamation is a strong statement. It shows shock or surprise. It may be a complete sentence or only part of a sentence.

EXAMPLES Your friends would be astounded!
An amazing thing to do!
Incredible!

EXERCISE 3 Number a sheet of paper 1–6. After each number, put the mark of end punctuation that goes with each sentence below.

1. This is absolutely crazy
2. Why must we put up with this monster
3. The other one gave us enough trouble
4. Is there any way to get rid of him
5. Try paying no attention
6. Get away from me

INSIDE PUNCTUATION

Certain marks of punctuation are used inside sentences. Most of these marks show separation of parts of the sentence.

The mark of inside punctuation used most often is the comma (,). The other marks, used less often, are the semicolon (;); the hyphen (-); the dash (—); and underlining. In printed material such as books, underlining is not used often. Instead, special letters called *italics* are used. The word *italic* shows how the letters look in italic.

The Comma

10f A comma is used between items in a series.

See Phrase, p. 328; Clause, p. 313

A series is made up of three or more items. The items may be words, phrases, clauses, or numerals.

EXAMPLES In the cages you can see birds, monkeys, and seals.
The birds fly across the cages, onto the perches, and against the wire screen.
Monkeys sleep at night, owls hunt after dark, and wildcats sleep or hunt in the day or the night.
The lock works with the combination numbers 3, 16, and 3.

Note: Sometimes the comma may be omitted between the last two items in a series. Follow your teacher's instruction.

EXERCISE 4 The following sentences are missing commas. Number a sheet of paper 1–8 and write the words just before and after a missing comma. Put a comma between them.

EXAMPLE A computer is a fast efficient and inexpensive machine for solving problems.

fast, efficient, and

1. Computers are used in government farming and business.
2. They are also used in education scientific research and engineering projects.
3. In government, computers deal with facts about people finances and materials.
4. Business computers keep track of sales, customer payments, and the amount of goods stored in warehouses.

5. Scientists use computers for measuring giant quantities such as the size and weight of the earth the amount of heat on the sun's surface or the distance across our galaxy.
6. They also use them to measure the tiniest forces of an atom the energy of a worm crawling or the strength of a butterfly's wing.
7. Engineers use computers to help design buildings bridges and dams.
8. Some computers need a large room to hold them some fit in a person's hand but many fit on a desk or table.

10g Commas are used to set off items that interrupt a sentence.

Items that interrupt a sentence are extra words or phrases.

EXAMPLES Blackstone, *the famous magician*, amazed his audiences with his tricks.
My uncle, *having no magical talent*, amazed no one.
My aunt, *however*, amazed everyone.

(1) Commas are used to set off appositives.

An *appositive* is a word or phrase that repeats the meaning of another word or phrase it follows. An appositive is set off from the rest of the sentence with commas because it interrupts the flow of a sentence.

EXAMPLES Hubert, *our dog*, has a strange personality.
When he sees our neighbor's cat, *Skipper*, he turns and runs.

EXERCISE 5 Write the following sentences. Put in commas where they are missing.

EXAMPLE Tasmania a large island is south of Australia.
Tasmania, a large island, is south of Australia.

1. Tasmania is the home of the shearwater a sea bird.
2. Some shearwaters also live near Adelaide a city in South Australia.
3. The shearwater a kind of albatross raises its young along the seashore.
4. Grown shearwaters leave their homes in April the end of the Tasmanian summer.
5. They begin their annual migration a fantastic journey.
6. They fly northeast nearly two thousand miles, passing Auckland a seaport in New Zealand.
7. Then they fly north toward Wake Island a lonely Pacific sandspit.
8. Turning northwest, they skirt Japan and then head for Alaska their destination.
9. By August the end of Alaska's summer they start back to Tasmania.
10. They fly along North America's west coast and across the Pacific to complete their migration a journey of 24,000 miles.

(2) Commas are used to set off words like *yes, no,* and *well* when they interrupt a sentence.

EXAMPLES Say, do you think she forgot us?
No, she said she would be here.
Well, how long should we wait?

(3) Commas are used to set off transitional terms.

Transitional terms like *however* and *nevertheless* help to show the continuing thought from sentence to sentence. A transitional term serves as a bridge from one thought to another. Transitional terms are not part of the main thought of a sentence. This is why they should be set off with commas.

EXAMPLES I know you want to stay here. *Nevertheless*, I think we should all go. You could, *of course*, join us later. *However*, you might get lost.

(4) Commas are used to set off names used in a direct address.

EXAMPLES Could you tell me, *sir*, how to reach Elm Street?
Dave, I hope you know what you are doing.

EXERCISE 6 Some of the following sentences need commas. Write correctly each sentence needing a comma. Write *C* if a sentence needs no comma.

EXAMPLE Ms. Okada my favorite teacher just telephoned.

Ms. Okada, my favorite teacher, just telephoned.

1. Stringbean Tomasino needs no introduction to you.
2. Nevertheless I want to say a few words about him.
3. He is of course an expert on vegetables.
4. Well if he is not an expert, at least he knows what he likes.
5. His favorite vegetable is of all things rutabaga.
6. However he saves room for parsnips and Chinese cabbage.
7. Could you tell us Stringbean what else you eat?
8. Say where did he go?

(5) Commas are used to set off nonessential word groups.

A nonessential phrase or clause gives additional information about someone or something. It is not needed to make the main thought of a sentence clear.

EXAMPLE Tom Hunter learned to wrestle bears.

Tom Hunter, *hoping to make money*, learned to wrestle bears.

[The phrase *hoping to make money* is not necessary to make the meaning of the sentence clear. It is an added phrase that gives extra information about Tom Hunter. Therefore, it is set off by commas.]

An essential phrase or clause, however, is not set off with commas.

EXAMPLE The bear that broke Tom's arm was the last one he wrestled.
[The clause *that broke Tom's arm* is needed to identify which bear was the last he wrestled.]

Here are more examples of the punctuation of nonessential and essential word groups.

NONESSENTIAL Her left hand, burned by the steam, was turning red.

ESSENTIAL The hand burned by the steam was turning red.

NONESSENTIAL Those tiny onions, fresh from the garden, can be eaten raw.

ESSENTIAL Onions that are fresh can be eaten raw.

Hint: If you can omit the phrase or clause in a sentence and still read the sentence with no possible confusion, the phrase or clause is *nonessential*. It should be set off with commas.

EXERCISE 7 Some of the following sentences contain nonessential clauses or phrases. Rewrite each sentence with a nonessential phrase or clause. Add commas where they belong.

EXAMPLE The fire which was burning briskly made a cheery picture in the room.

The fire, which was burning briskly, made a cheery picture in the room.

1. Tabby asleep on the rug seemed barely to breathe.
2. A slight wind which had only just started moaned softly around the cabin.
3. The light from two lamps which Molly had lit gave a pale light.
4. The lamp on the mantle flickered low.
5. The other lamp resting on the table at Molly's elbow shed a brighter light.
6. Molly hoping to finish early made her fingers fly at her work.
7. Suddenly the old clock on the mantle struck its bell.
8. Molly not wanting to lose time never looked up.

10h A comma is used to separate adjectives not joined by the conjunction *and*.

EXAMPLES She picked up the *broken*, *twisted* fork.

She let it fall to the floor with a *hollow*, *toneless* clatter.

Do not, however, put a comma between adjectives if the second adjective is closely connected to the noun.

EXAMPLE The *old plow* horse had been retired for years.
[No comma is needed because the adjective *plow* is closely connected to *horse.*]

EXERCISE 8 The following sentences need commas. Number a sheet of paper 1–6. Next to each number, write the word before and after a comma that belongs in the sentence. Put in the missing comma.

EXAMPLE A locust is a hungry troublesome pest.
hungry, troublesome

1. Locusts travel in large sweeping swarms.
2. Sometimes these swarms grow into huge dark clouds ten miles wide.
3. Locusts land in a field as a crackling seething mass.
4. A thick hungry swarm can eat two thousand tons of food a day.
5. They will eat all green living vegetation in sight.
6. When they go, they leave a dull barren landscape.

10i A comma is used to set off a dependent clause that begins a sentence.

See Clause, p. 313

A dependent clause has a subject and verb. It usually begins with a word such as *after, before, because, if,* or *when.*

When a dependent clause begins a sentence, it should be set off with a comma.

EXAMPLES *After she had eaten breakfast,* she felt like going back to bed.
If everyone did that, the pace of living might slow down.
Whenever she feels too energetic, she rests until the feeling goes away.

EXERCISE 9 Each of the following sentences needs a comma. Number a sheet of paper 1–6. After each number, write the words before and after the place for a comma. Write in the comma.

EXAMPLE If you look closely at the trees you can see the butterflies.
trees, you

1. If you have been to Monterey in winter you may have seen the butterfly trees.
2. When you inspect these trees you notice sleeping butterflies hanging in the branches.
3. Although these Monarch butterflies look like a part of the tree one can see them clearly up close.
4. After they leave Canada in the fall they migrate to this region.
5. Even though a Monarch weighs only as much as a small paper clip it flies over two thousand miles a year.
6. If it has worked that hard it deserves a quiet sleep in the trees.

10j A comma is used before a coordinating conjunction joining independent clauses in a compound sentence.

See Conjunction, p. 316

Wherever a coordinating conjunction joins the clauses of a compound sentence, put a comma in front of the conjunction.

EXAMPLES Lincoln thought the Confederate Army would not attack, *but* Lee led his men directly into battle.
The boat was lowered into the water, *and* Captain Cox ordered the men over the side.

Note: Short clauses in a compound sentence usually do not need a comma before the coordinating conjunction. Follow your teacher's instruction.

EXAMPLE The leader fell but she leaped up.

EXERCISE 10 Each of the following sentences needs a comma. Number a sheet of paper 1–8. After each number, write the words before and after the place for a comma. Write in the comma.

EXAMPLE All kinds of fish migrate to lay eggs but Pacific salmon are somewhat unusual.
eggs, but

1. The Pacific salmon is born in fresh water but it spends most of its life in the ocean.
2. An adult salmon must return from the ocean to fresh water for it lays its eggs there.

3. Salmon eggs grow in fresh water but they will die if transferred to salt water too soon.
4. The adult salmon swims upstream in rivers and it will not stop until it reaches the headwaters.
5. Salmon struggle hard to get upstream for they seem to know where they are going.
6. The salmon eat during the early part of their upstream journey but near the end they stop eating.
7. Their stomachs shrink like a balloon losing air and their throats close.
8. They have come to lay their eggs and then the worn out salmon quietly die.

10k Commas are used in certain standard forms.

(1) Commas are used with quotation marks around the words of a speaker.

EXAMPLE Wally called out, "We're coming," as he struggled into his coat.

Notice that commas separate the quoted words from the name of the speaker and anything said about the speaker. The comma comes before the quotation marks.

EXAMPLES She said, "Start the motor."
"I'm trying to," he answered.

EXERCISE 11 Write each of the following sentences on a sheet of paper. Insert commas where they belong.

EXAMPLE "Come out of there" called Tom.

"Come out of there," called Tom.

1. Tom turned to Becky and asked "Are you all right?"
2. "I'm fine" she answered.
3. "Well, hurry" Tom panted "or he'll catch us."
4. Becky stopped and asked Tom "Is that the way?"
5. "I think it is" he said, looking around in the gloom "because I remember that rock ledge."
6. Becky stood still and said "I think we'd better go this way."
7. As she turned, Tom came after her saying "You're right, Becky."
8. He was quiet another few seconds and then added "If we get out alive, it'll be you that saved us."

(2) Commas are used to separate items in dates and geographical names.

EXAMPLE Early settlers founded Detroit, Michigan, on July 24, 1701.

A comma is also used to separate dates and geographical names from the rest of the sentence.

EXAMPLE He was born on September 20, 1946, in Boston.

EXERCISE 12 Number a sheet of paper 1–4. Next to each number, write each part of the following items that need commas. Add commas where they belong.

EXAMPLE Babe Ruth was born on February 6 1895.

February 6, 1895

1. The famous composer Franz Schubert was born in Vienna Austria on January 31 1797.
2. His well-known *Unfinished Symphony* was never played until December 17 1865 thirty-seven years after his death.
3. The *Constitution,* called *Old Ironsides,* was launched in Boston Massachusetts on October 21 1797.
4. James Buchanan, our fifteenth president, was born in a log cabin April 23 1791 near Mercersburg Pa.

(3) A comma is used after the greeting and the closing in a friendly letter.

The standard form of a friendly letter is shown here.

5 Deerfield Lane South
Pleasantville, New York 10570
March 12, 1983

Dear Aunt Susan,

Guess what! We have a new baby brother. His name is David. Mom says he looks like Dad. I guess so, but I really can't tell it.

Right now he is sleeping in my room, but he doesn't do enough of it as far as I am concerned! Oh well, I guess I will be glad to have him a dozen years from now or so.

Thank you for asking me to come to Macomb this summer. I would love to do that. I'll help you with Andrea and Deckman. I hope you will teach me how to make more of those yummy cookies we made last year.

Mom is calling me for dinner so I'll stop writing. Give my best to everyone, including Rebel.

My best,

Dina

REVIEW EXERCISES for Punctuation are found at the end of Chapter 11.

CHAPTER

11

PUNCTUATION

Semicolons, Colons, Hyphens, Apostrophes, Quotation Marks, Italics, Parentheses

This chapter deals with marks of inside punctuation that are used to separate the parts of a sentence: *semicolons, colons, hyphens,* and *apostrophes.* Several marks of enclosing punctuation—*quotation marks, italics,* and *parentheses*—are also introduced here.

INSIDE PUNCTUATION

The Semicolon

See Compound Sentence, p. 315

See Conjunction, p. 316

11a A semicolon is used between the clauses in a compound sentence that are not joined by a conjunction.

EXAMPLES Some Native Americans settled in a forest; others moved about on the open plains.

Natives in the northern and southern parts of the continents adapted to the cold; those in the central parts became accustomed to hot weather.

The semicolon works like a strong comma. It marks the joining of two long independent clauses.

11b A semicolon is used between the clauses in a compound sentence when either clause has a comma in it.

EXAMPLES Ruby Nogata decided not to take the bus; instead, she walked the six blocks to the depot.

The orchestra played waltzes, foxtrots, and polkas; but the young people had come to hear rock and roll.

EXERCISE 1 The following sentences are missing semicolons. Number a sheet of paper 1–6. Next to each number, write the words that come before and after the place where a semicolon belongs. Put in a semicolon.

EXAMPLE European eels spend most of their lives in fresh water however, they travel to the Atlantic Ocean to lay their eggs.

water; however

1. The Sargasso Sea near Bermuda is two thousand miles from Europe nevertheless, eels from Europe swim there to lay eggs.
2. The eels lay their eggs deep down in the Sargasso Sea then they die.
3. They never return to the rivers of Europe however, their eggs hatch into tiny, ribbon-like fish.
4. These little creatures, feeding and growing, drift and swim with the Gulf Stream but it is about three years before they reach the shores of Europe.
5. There they turn into small, transparent eels, known as glass eels and they start their trip up the very same river their parents left.
6. How the baby eels know where to go is a mystery however, their long migrations are now known to scientists.

The Colon

11c A colon is used to introduce a list of items.

EXAMPLES These are the beverages available: milk, buttermilk, lemonade, and iced tea.

The only seats left are the following ones: 12a, 12b, 13a, 13d, and 14a.

11d A colon is used in numerals expressing time.

EXAMPLES 8:30 A.M.
It was 4:15 in the afternoon.

EXERCISE 2 Write the following sentences on a sheet of paper. Put in colons where they belong.

EXAMPLE Officer Starrett listed the following items a belt, a pair of handcuffs, and a whistle.

Officer Starrett listed the following items: a belt, a pair of handcuffs, and a whistle.

1. She arrived at 1015 P.M.
2. These groceries were on the shopping list cereal, milk, and sugar.
3. Jenny started her business promptly at 905 A.M.
4. Is 1200 A.M. at midnight or noon?
5. Add these to your camping list dried beans, raisins, and nuts.

The Hyphen

11e A hyphen is used to connect the parts of certain compound words and word numbers from twenty-one to ninety-nine.

EXAMPLES daughter-in-law
push-ups
The weigh-in station
ninety-nine (but not numbers greater)

Certain compound words do not take hyphens.

EXAMPLES salesclerk
midnight

If you are in doubt about a word, look it up in a dictionary.

11f A hyphen is used to divide a word at the end of a line.

EXAMPLE General Washington, this is indeed a revolutionary plan.

Be sure to divide words between syllables, not in the middle of a syllable.

WRONG With the framing of our Constitution, our Founding Fathers gave
us a national purpose.

RIGHT With the framing of our Constitution, our Founding Fathers gave
us a national purpose.

EXERCISE 3 Number a sheet of paper 1–10. Copy each of the following items. Write the syllables separately and put in hyphens between them. You may use a dictionary.

EXAMPLE gathering

gath-er-ing

1. demonstrate
2. son in law
3. television
4. manufacture
5. government
6. forty three
7. election
8. transportation
9. secondary
10. pull ups

The Apostrophe

11g An apostrophe is used with nouns to show possession or close relationship.

See Possessive, p. 328

EXAMPLES Please pick up your sister's glove.
Winter's storms are upon us.
The magazine's cover made me laugh.

(1) Most singular nouns form the possessive with an apostrophe and an *s*.

EXAMPLES cat's cradle
Morton's handlebars
one minute's worth of work

(2) A plural noun ending in *s* forms the possessive with an apostrophe only.

EXAMPLES The cars' exhaust fumes discolor air.
The bees' humming kept me awake.

(3) A plural noun not ending in *s* adds an apostrophe and an *s*.

EXAMPLES The men's club opened its doors to women.
The women's rights were met.

EXERCISE 4 Some of the following sentences are correct. Others have errors in the use of the apostrophe to show possession. On a sheet of paper write *C* for any sentence that is correct. Copy any incorrect sentence. Write it with the correct use of the apostrophe.

EXAMPLE The cars' horn was stuck.

The car's horn was stuck.

1. The highway's outside lane was crowded.
2. A detectives' car had stalled.
3. The commuters' tempers were short.
4. Their car's radiators were steaming.
5. The suns' heat was unbearable.
6. One drivers' anger made him push hard on his horn.
7. Its blast got on other persons' nerves.
8. A commuter's life is not a happy one.

11h An apostrophe is used to show that letters have been omitted.

EXAMPLES		
	hasn't (has not)	he'll (he will)
	don't (do not)	haven't (have not)
	I'll (I will)	won't (will not)

The above examples with apostrophes are *contractions.* A contraction is a word made by combining two words and omitting some letters. An apostrophe is used to show where letters have been omitted.

See Common Confusions, p. 180 and p. 188

Note: *It's* is a contraction of *it is*. *It's* does not show possession.
Who's is a contraction of *who is*. *Who's* does not show possession.

EXERCISE 5 Number a sheet of paper 1–10. Rewrite the following items. Put in apostrophes where they belong.

EXAMPLE Whos that?

Who's that?

1. doesnt
2. wont
3. Its all right.
4. the boys club
5. havent
6. the womens entry
7. Whos going to meet us?
8. hadnt
9. Can you be sure its safe?
10. Well soon know whos right

Italics (the underline)

11i Underlining is used for titles of books, movies, periodicals, ships, letters of the alphabet, and important works created by people. In printed material, these items are set in italics.

EXAMPLES The *National Geographic* had a picture of the sailing ship *Yankee Clipper.*

Frankenstein was a book long before it was made into a movie.

EXERCISE 6 Words in the following sentences need underlining. Number a sheet of paper 1–5. Next to each number, write the word or words in the sentence that need underlining. Underline the words you write.

EXAMPLE Joshua Slocum sailed alone around the world on his ship named the Spray.

Spray

1. There now are two movies titled King Kong.
2. Our first atomic submarine was named Nautilus.
3. All persons whose last names begin with M should be in line.
4. I like Rodin's statue The Thinker very much.
5. People magazine sells on the newsstands.

ENCLOSING PUNCTUATION

Marks of enclosing punctuation come before and after written material. Enclosing punctuation shows that the material enclosed is special in nature. The enclosing punctuation marks in this section are *quotation marks* and *parentheses*.

Quotation Marks

11j Quotation marks are used to enclose a speaker's exact words.

EXAMPLES "The sky is falling," said Henry.
Belle answered, "There's no place to hide."

Only the direct quotation needs quotation marks. An indirect quotation does not. An indirect quotation is a rewording of a speaker's words.

DIRECT QUOTATION "I'll be on time," said Ginny.

INDIRECT QUOTATION Ginny said she would be on time.

11k Single quotation marks are used to enclose a quotation within a quotation.

EXAMPLES "I'm sure I heard you say, 'Stop,' when I moved," said Vickie.

"No," said Ms. Cherney, "I said 'Start,' but you went too soon."

11l Quotation marks are used to enclose titles of chapters, articles, short stories, poems, songs, and other short pieces of writing.

EXAMPLES Objects in the sky appear in many song titles such as "When You Wish Upon a Star," "Blue Moon," and "Over the Rainbow."

"The Ransom of Red Chief" is the story of a naughty boy.

Clement Moore's poem "The Night Before Christmas" was written in the nineteenth century.

11m A period always goes inside the end quotation marks.

A question mark or an exclamation mark goes inside the quotation marks if the quotation itself is a question or an exclamation. Otherwise, these marks go outside the quotation marks.

EXAMPLES "Should I put the hinge pin in before I hang the door?" asked Walter.
"Put the door up first!" yelled Carey.
Did he say, "Put the door up first"?

EXERCISE 7 Some of the following sentences need single or double quotation marks. On your paper write each sentence needing quotation marks. Put in the quotation marks where they belong.

EXAMPLE Didi said, I like that music.
Didi said, "I like that music."

1. Who's singing that? asked Rachel.
2. Didi answered, I think it's Winnie Sommer.
3. Is Winnie her real name? asked Carl.
4. Didi told him it was a nickname.
5. Then what's her real name? asked Carl.
6. It's something different, was her answer.
7. Did you say different? asked Rachel.
8. Didi told her, I saw her name printed. It's Wintra.
9. Didi added that she was not sure.
10. Carl laughed, That would make her cold and hot because her name is Wintra Sommer.

EXERCISE 8 On your paper rewrite each of the following. Rewrite each indirect quotation to make it a direct quotation. Add the correct quotation marks. Rewrite each direct quotation to make it an indirect quotation. Take out the unnecessary quotation marks.

EXAMPLE "Monty, have you read any books by Judy Blume?" asked Todd.

Todd asked Monty if he had read any books by Judy Blume.

1. "No," answered Monty, "but my sister has."
2. Todd asked what book she liked.
3. "She likes them all," said Monty.
4. "Why do you ask me?" continued Monty.
5. "Blume knows about girls," said Todd.
6. "If you want to find out more about girls, read a book by Blume," Todd went on.

Parentheses

11n Parentheses are used to enclose extra items added in a sentence.

EXAMPLE The French celebrate Bastille Day (similar to the Fourth of July) on the fourteenth of July.

REVIEW EXERCISE A End Punctuation

The following paragraphs are written without end punctuation. Decide where each sentence should end. On a sheet of paper rewrite the paragraphs. Add all the end punctuation and circle it.

One morning Mr. Cosmo found a small wooden box at his front door he took it in, looked it over carefully, and set it down on a table he forgot about the box for several weeks then one night he had an odd experience.

As he was reading, he noticed a movement on the table he looked closely a thin boy's hand was slowly coming out of the box the nails on the hand were long and black

For a moment he was afraid would he have the strength to destroy that horrible hand what enemy had sent him the mysterious box he threw his book at the hand and shouted, "Get out" the hand vanished perhaps his eyes had deceived him would he ever know

REVIEW EXERCISE B **Commas**

Copy the following sentences on a sheet of paper. Add commas where they are needed and circle them.

1. When he was sixty-five years old Benjamin Franklin began to write his autobiography.
2. He wrote it especially for his son William governor of New Jersey.
3. Franklin had been a printer an inventor a politician and a writer.
4. He is of course best remembered as a politician.
5. Franklin's father a dyer was born in Ecton England.
6. Franklin's father taught his children six boys and four girls to think and talk at the dinner table.

7. Franklin liked good food but he thought that good talk was even more important than good food.
8. He was in fact an excellent talker.
9. When he went to France the French women found him charming.
10. When President Washington thanked Franklin for his service to the United States Franklin said "Sir I was honored to serve my country."

REVIEW EXERCISE C Essential and Nonessential Clauses and Phrases

Number a sheet of paper 1–10. After each number, tell whether the underlined clause or phrase is *essential* or *nonessential*. If the underlined part of the sentence is not essential, show how the sentence should be punctuated.

EXAMPLE Every student whose hair is green will be given an *A*.

essential

Marie Silva whose hair is green is gentle and kind.

nonessential, Marie Silva, whose hair is green, is gentle and kind.

1. The dinner that Diana had last Thanksgiving was the best she had ever eaten.
2. The turkey which was a twenty-pound hen was roasted until it was tender and juicy.
3. Diana's mother who has taught her how to cook had prepared mashed potatoes and gravy.

4. Diana poured the gravy which was rich, smooth, and delicious into a huge dent in her mountain of potatoes.
5. The turkey dressing that her mother makes is Diana's favorite.
6. It is crunchy with chestnuts that Diana's uncle brings in from his ranch.
7. Diana's cousin who usually eats only desserts ate three helpings of turkey and potatoes.
8. He even ate the vegetables which were attractively arranged on his plate.
9. The dessert that Diana's mother served was a pumpkin pie topped with whipped cream.
10. Diana and her cousin agreed that people who have eaten too much dinner have a hard time eating pumpkin pie and whipped cream.

REVIEW EXERCISE D Review of Punctuation

Copy the following sentences on a sheet of paper. Add all of the needed punctuation and circle it. Do not use periods.

EXAMPLE My grandmother a fortuneteller was born at Dunbar Nebraska.

My grandmother, a fortuneteller, was born at Dunbar, Nebraska.

1. Benny my brother always reads the horoscope in the *Daily News*.
2. He says that he does not believe in the horoscopes he is just curious about them.

3. Our sister who is a Leo always asks Benny to read the daily horoscope for Leos.
4. When her horoscope said that she would be lucky she entered a spelling contest at school but she misspelled the first word.
5. Benny said Sis how could you misspell a word on your lucky day.
6. Its easy to see that the horoscope was wrong my sister answered.
7. Instead of depending upon the stars or that silly misleading horoscope for help she decided to study her spelling lesson.
8. Because her horoscope said that she would make new friends my sister waited all day for the doorbell to ring but no one ever came.
9. However she did have one correct horoscope.
10. One unlucky day she lost her homework paper fell down the front steps of the school and got home too late to watch her favorite television program.

REVIEW EXERCISE E Review of Punctuation

Copy the following letter on a sheet of paper. Punctuate the letter correctly and circle the punctuation.

1815 Waterloo Road
Oakland California
July 14 19_ _

Dear Harriet

Last night I read a story that reminded me of our fun together last summer. The story was The Mystery of the Haunted House. Do you remember the haunted house at Disneyland? When you fell through the trap door I was afraid I would never see you again. Then a soft cool cloth brushed over my face. I was sure it was a ghost a goblin or even a ghoul. Well I like to read about haunted houses but Ill never go in one again I hope.

I do wish I could see you again this summer though. Because youre athletic you would enjoy joining me in my lessons. Im taking the following classes gymnastics ballet and soccer. The gymnastics coach a champion gymnast was in the Olympics in 1972. Her picture was in Sports Illustrated that year, too. She amazes me by doing fifty five push ups in one minute. She says theres nothing to it but nevertheless I admire her for her strength and endurance.

Before I start back to school Im going to see an old movie Star Wars.

Thats all there is to my summer Harriet. Write to tell me about yours.

Your friend
Julie

REVIEW EXERCISE F **Vocabulary**

Review the following words:

atmosphere	ghost
avalanche	ghoul
besiege	hazardous
disaster	horoscope
expedition	mysterious

Number a separate sheet of paper 1–3. Combine each of the pairs of sentences into one sentence, either by using a semicolon or by changing one independent clause to a dependent clause.

EXAMPLE Abe's horoscope said that he would have an accident on Tuesday. The horoscope was wrong.

Although Abe's horoscope said that he would have an accident on Tuesday, the horoscope was wrong.

1. The Arctic expedition was besieged by disasters. One member of the expedition was killed in an avalanche.
2. The atmosphere in the classroom was tense. The teacher was giving a surprise quiz.
3. The words *ghost* and *ghoul* both begin with *gh*. Both words name creatures who might be found in a cemetery.

UNIT FIVE

AIDS AND ENRICHMENT

Speaking and Listening
Spelling
Sources of Information

CHAPTER

12

SPEAKING AND LISTENING

Speech is the simplest way for people to share ideas. People usually learn to speak at an early age. They keep on speaking all their lives.

Listening goes with speaking. In fact, an individual learns to speak by listening first. Both speaking and listening go on most of a person's life.

Good speaking and listening cannot be learned in a short time. These skills must be practiced in many different situations before they will improve. You may find it helpful to follow the rules for speaking and listening that are described in this chapter.

INFORMAL CONVERSATION

12a Think before you speak.

Are you applying brain power to word power? Or do you let your words pour out without thinking? The words you speak should accurately tell what is going on inside your mind.

Do you know what the purpose of your words is? Thinking about how you want to influence your listener will help you take part in a conversation. When you speak informally, make it a habit to think before you speak. Some simple rules will help you develop better speaking habits. Here are three main rules.

(1) Talk about what will interest your listener.

Think about things your listener is interested in. No one will want to hold a conversation with you if he or she is not interested in what you have to say. Your listener is most likely to listen if you are talking about something of special interest.

If you do not know what your listener is interested in, it is up to you to find out. Ask a question. Of course, it probably will do little good to ask point blank, "What are you interested in?"

It is better to comment on something that interests you that you think will also interest your listener. Then ask a question about the other person's interest in that topic.

EXAMPLE "I really like (name of something—a new car, a sport, a show, a kind of clothing, a musical group). Who (or what) do you think is the best?"

(2) Ask questions to give the other person a chance to talk.

Even if you are talking about a subject that interests your listener, you need to give him or her a chance to join in the conversation. Listening is just one part of conversation.

The quickest way to involve your listener is to ask a question. This way, he or she feels that the conversation is not all one-sided. There can be a sharing of ideas and opinions.

Here are some examples of the kinds of questions you can ask to involve others in a conversation:

"Did you do anything new this last vacation?"

"I've got a new recording of (name of song). Have you heard it?"

"I really like (name of a TV show). Do you have a favorite?"

"I'm having trouble keeping up with the assignments we get in (name of class). Do you have any tips you can give me for getting ahead?"

(3) Listen to and look at the person who is talking.

Being a good listener in a conversation is just as important as speaking. Keep track of the points being made. Look at the person speaking. Nod once in a while or say "yes" quietly. Do this to show you are following what is being said. Avoid interrupting the person who is speaking. Wait for a reasonable break in the flow of conversation. Then add your comments or ask a question.

12b Speak and listen the way you want others to speak and listen to you.

This is the Golden Rule of conversation. You can usually judge what others like in a conversation by thinking of what you like. Follow the Golden Rule of speaking and listening so that both you and others will enjoy carrying on a conversation.

EXERCISE 1 Play the role of the speaker or the listener in one of the following situations.

1. You are sitting in the stands at half-time of an athletic contest. A classmate who is new to school stops and says, "Hi." You begin a conversation.
2. While shopping in a store with a member of your family, you meet a classmate you hardly know. The classmate is with a parent who already knows your parent. They engage in conversation. You and the classmate also talk.
3. The first meeting of a school club has been called off, but you and another student do not know that. You both arrive at the meeting place at the same time, but no one else comes. You do not know the other student well.
4. You arrive at a neighbor's house to babysit for the first time there. Upstairs the parents are getting their young child ready for bed. A son (or daughter) who is a bit older than you is there, waiting to go out with the parents. You have not met before. You begin to converse.

INTRODUCTIONS

People you know who are with you but do not know each other are at some disadvantage. Each person would like to know who the other person is. You can help by introducing them to each other.

12c Introduce people who do not know each other.

Here are some basic ways to introduce people:

"I'd like you to meet (name)."
"Let me introduce (name)."
"May I introduce (name)?"
"I'm not sure you've met. This is (name)."

These introductions are somewhat formal. If the situation is less formal, you can say something simpler. For example, you might say, "This is (name)." Or just give the names of the two people.

When saying the name of one person, look at the person you tell it to. This way, the name of the person can be heard. Then look at the other person and say the name of the first person.

Examples of informal introductions:

(You are introducing two students, Jim Waring and Lily Manero.) Look at Lily and say, "Lily, this is Jim Waring." Then look at Jim and say, "This is Lily Manero."

(You are introducing a student, Nick Hess, to a teacher, Mrs. Haldi.) Look at the teacher and say, "Mrs. Haldi, I'd like you to meet Nick Hess." Then look at Nick and say, "Nick, Mrs. Haldi."

12d When one person you are introducing deserves special respect, mention that person's name first.

EXAMPLES "Dr. Thomas, I'd like to have you meet my friend Carol Wilder."
"Carol, this is Dr. Thomas."

"Mr. Goldfarb, may I introduce Ricky Swain."
"Ricky, this is Mr. Goldfarb."

The purpose of an introduction is to allow individuals to carry on a conversation. It is important that people who are introduced learn each other's names. If you are making the introduction, speak clearly the names of the people you are introducing.

EXERCISE 2 Take roles in the following situations.

1. A new neighbor has called on your family. You answer the door and learn his or her name. You introduce the other members of your family.
2. You are at a local fair with members of your family. The vice-principal from your school sees you and comes over to greet you. You introduce the vice-principal to your family.
3. An adult volunteer for a local charity or medical drive calls at your home. You answer the door. You learn the name of the volunteer. Then you introduce members of your family to the volunteer.
4. Adult friends are visiting in your home. A new friend of yours arrives. Introduce your friend to your family and your visitors.

12e When you are being introduced, listen closely to the name of the person new to you.

It is easy to miss hearing the names of people being introduced to you. Pay close attention to the name of each person. If you do not hear a name, it is all right to ask that it be repeated.

EXAMPLES "I didn't hear your name. Would you tell me again, please?"

"Excuse me, I missed hearing your name. Would you repeat it for me?"

"I'm sorry, I missed your name."

Whenever you hear the name of the person introduced to you, repeat it in your first response. Repeating it will help you to remember it.

EXAMPLES

FORMAL "I'm pleased to meet you, Dr. Stanislavsky."

INFORMAL "Hi, Jack. Good to meet you."

EXERCISE 3 Take a role with classmates in the following situations.

1. You introduce a classmate to your mother.
2. You introduce a classmate to the father of a friend.
3. You introduce your uncle to the school principal.
4. You introduce a friend to the owner of a local store.
5. You introduce a new classmate to a friend.

USING THE TELEPHONE

The telephone is an extension of speaking and listening. However, it has one major difference from face-to-face conversation.

In face-to-face conversation, people use more than just their voices to communicate. The look of the eye, the facial expression, a nod of the head, or a movement of the hands—all these enter into direct conversation. These aids are absent during a telephone conversation. This fact places an extra responsibility on the speaker to use his or her voice clearly in speaking on the telephone.

12f Use the telephone wisely.

(1) Plan ahead for the call you are making.

Be sure you have the right number. Think through the points you want to communicate. Avoid embarrassing yourself by having to admit on the telephone that you forgot what you were going to tell the other person.

When the other person answers your ring, state your name immediately.

EXAMPLES

INFORMAL "Hi, Ginger. This is (your name)."

FORMAL "Hello, Mr. Odum. This is (your name)."

If the person you want does not answer, ask, "May I speak with ______?" Or, "I'd like to speak with ______, please." If the person you are calling is not there, leave your name and number. If you want to leave a message, make it short and clear. Do not try to leave a long message for someone else to give to the person you called. Long messages are difficult to take on the phone and are easily confused. Instead, have the person you tried to reach call you back.

(2) Take calls efficiently.

If the incoming call is from someone known to you, identify yourself. Have pencil and paper near so that you can take notes if necessary. If the call is for someone else in your house, tell the caller whether or not that person is at home. If the person is away, tell the caller approximately when he or she is expected to return. Ask if there is any message. Make notes of the information the caller gives you. Note the time the call came in, the name of the caller, the number to call back, and other basic information.

FORMAL SPEAKING AND LISTENING

On occasion you will be expected to speak to a group of people. This calls for a more formal manner of speaking than a conversation.

12g Use formal language when speaking to a group.

In class, at a club meeting, or in some other group situation, formal language works better than informal language. Informal or casual language is all right for conversation with one or two friends.

But if you want a group to take what you say seriously, you need to choose your words carefully.

To make your talk successful, plan ahead. Learn how to prepare a talk. Learn the techniques for delivering it.

12h Prepare your talk in advance.

Think carefully about information for your topic, the main idea of your talk. Search out any additional information you need. Take notes on the information you know or find. Then organize those notes into three parts.

The first part will be your *beginning*. Think of this as an introduction to the topic. The second part will be your *middle,* or central part. This is the body of your talk. The third part will be your *ending*. The final part of your talk concludes what you have to say.

To prepare thoroughly, you will want to follow seven steps.

1. Choose a topic you know about or can find out about.
2. Choose a topic that will interest most of your listeners.
3. Choose a topic that you can present in the time allowed.
4. Find out more information than you can use in your report.
5. Select the information that will mean the most to your listeners.

6. Organize your information in three main parts: the introduction, the body, and the conclusion.
7. Practice giving the report out loud by referring only to your notes.

Outlining

One of the best ways to write notes is in the form of an outline. An outline may be in standard form. The standard outline follows a form like this:

I. (First main point)
    A. (First subpoint)
        1. (First supporting detail, if any)
        2. (Second supporting detail, if any)
    B. (Second subpoint)
II. (Second main point)
    A. (First subpoint)
    B. (Second subpoint)
III. (Final main point)

Each main point is supported by sub-points and supporting details. The relationships are shown clearly by the indentions and the use of Roman numerals, capital letters, and Arabic numerals.

Delivering Your Talk

12i Deliver your talk the way you would want to listen to it.

(1) Speak clearly.

Make it a practice to talk clearly to the person in your audience farthest away from you. By doing this, you make sure that all your audience hears you. Avoid mumbling or slurring your words. Speak so that the people in the back of the room do not have to strain to understand what you say.

(2) Speak to your listeners.

Look directly at your listeners. Pick out one or two in the back of the room to look at from time to time. Pick out one or two on each side to look at, also. It is expected that you will look at your notes, but look up at your listeners, too.

(3) Keep your body still except to make a point.

Whenever you move, your motion attracts the attention of your audience. If you wiggle, shuffle your feet, or scratch your head, this motion will take attention away from what you are saying. You should move only when you want to make a special point. Then, a short motion with the open hand is often enough. Work to keep from making unnecessary motions.

(4) Appear at your best.

Look pleasant, and your audience will feel pleasant about you. Look unhappy, and your audience will be unhappy, too. Smile once in a while, especially at the beginning and end of your talk. Dress neatly. In short, do all you can to appear at your best.

(5) Avoid useless words and sounds.

Words or sounds that do not add to your talk should be avoided. In conversation, many people add a "you know" or "I mean" to their statements. These additions may be all right in conversation, but in a formal talk, they draw attention away from your message. Keep them out of your talk.

Keep your sentences on your topic. Make each sentence add something to your talk.

Too many extra sounds will also damage your talk. Avoid them. An "ah" here or an "um" there or too much clearing of the throat will interrupt the flow of your words.

12j Listen to another's talk as you want others to listen to yours.

Follow the Golden Rule when listening to a talk by someone else. Give your attention to the speaker. Do nothing that will distract either the speaker or other listeners around you. This means remaining quiet and paying attention to what the speaker has to say.

Take notes if you are expected to remember the points a speaker is making. Be sure, however, to take the notes in a way that will not disturb others. If you tear off a sheet of paper or crumple it, the noise will be a disturbance.

Just being quiet, of course, is not all there is to being a good listener. Your attention as well needs to be given to the speaker. Gazing out the window or reading a book at your seat while a speaker is giving a talk will take away from the success of the occasion.

Speaking and listening go together. Both are needed to make communication complete and successful.

REVIEW EXERCISE A Introductions

Take roles in the following situations.

1. An adult in your family visits one of your classes. You must introduce your teacher and the adult.
2. In a grocery store with your aunt, you meet the man who was your teacher in the sixth grade. You must introduce the teacher to your aunt.
3. A cousin of your own age is visiting from another state. You must introduce him or her to two of your friends.
4. You have invited a friend home to dinner. You must introduce your friend to the rest of your family.
5. You have an appointment with a dentist whose office you have never visited before. You must introduce yourself to the dentist or to the dentist's receptionist.

REVIEW EXERCISE B Using the Telephone

Take roles in the following situations using a telephone.

1. You are calling a friend to ask about a homework assignment. Your friend answers.

2. You are calling a friend to ask about a homework assignment. The friend's older sister answers and tells you that your friend is not at home. You leave a message.
3. You are calling a store to ask about an item that you have seen advertised in that day's newspaper.

REVIEW EXERCISE C Suiting the Topic to the Audience

Read the following two lists of topics and audiences. On a sheet of paper, list the topics. After each topic, write the letters of those audiences for which you would use the topic. Then tell whether the discussion would be formal or informal. Be prepared to explain your choices.

EXAMPLE The problems of having big feet

The problems of having big feet, C, informal

TOPICS	AUDIENCE
1. The story of Betsy Ross and the first flag	A. A prepared talk to a class
2. The most difficult position in baseball	B. A prepared talk to adults
3. The value of pets	C. An evening telephone conversation with a friend
4. Food in the school cafeteria	D. A conversation with a teacher
5. Personal experience of an accident	

REVIEW EXERCISE D **Topic and Audience**

Prepare a short speech on each of the following topics. Consider what to say to each of the two suggested listeners.

1. Explain the way from your class to the principal's office. Explain first to a student who knows the school. Then explain to a stranger at the school.
2. Explain why you have or have not enjoyed a particular film or television program. Explain first to a listener who has seen the film or the program. Then explain to a listener who has not seen the film or program.
3. Explain how to open your school locker. Explain first to another student in your school. Then explain to a listener who has never seen a locker.

REVIEW EXERCISE E **Outlining**

Read the following short speeches. On a sheet of paper, fill in the outline form that follows each speech.

Was Columbus the Last?

The first people to settle North America probably came from Asia across what is now Alaska. They used stone knives and axes and may have had dogs. Their descendants were the Indians of North and South America.

Norsemen also discovered this continent. Around the year 900, Eric the Red landed on

Greenland and built a settlement there. His son, Leif the Lucky, sailed from Greenland to the northeast coast of North America.

There may have been other discoveries of North America before Columbus' voyage in 1492. Therefore, we could say that Columbus was the last to discover America, but not the first.

Was Columbus the Last?

I.
  A.
  B.
  C.
II.
  A.
  B.
III.

A Vegetable Garden

To get fresh vegetables from your own garden, you as a gardener must plan ahead and work hard. First, you must order seeds from a good seed company. If you have grown vegetables before, you may get the best seeds from your own garden.

Before you can plant the seeds, you should turn up the soil with a spade or a plow. Then you should pulverize the spaded soil.

You must plan your garden. You must decide where each vegetable will be planted and how much space each crop will need. You might make a calendar and show on it the date for planting your spring crop and the date for planting your winter crop.

As the plants grow, the gardener who wants a good crop will fertilize the soil and water the plants regularly.

A Vegetable Garden

I.
- A.
- B.

II.
- A.
- B.

III.
- A.
- B.
  - 1.
  - 2.

IV.
- A.
- B.

REVIEW EXERCISE F **Vocabulary**

Review the following words. Look up the meaning or pronunciation of any unfamiliar words.

1. achievement
2. attendance
3. burglar
4. curriculum
5. discipline
6. nuisance
7. punctual
8. solar heat
9. suburban
10. virtue

Prepare a speech in which you use at least one of the words from the word list. Use the seven steps in preparing your speech. Be sure to have a clear topic sentence.

Suggestions: An undisciplined dog is a nuisance in an urban area.

The curriculum in a junior high school should include team sports with other schools for both boys and girls.

Students can learn about the real business world by taking part in Junior Achievement.

Attendance at the annual science fair should be voluntary for junior high school students.

CHAPTER

13

SPELLING

Nobody knows why some people find spelling hard. Even if spelling is hard for you, however, it can be made easier.

You can improve your spelling by learning basic rules. Spelling rules are not like laws that must be obeyed. They are guides that will help you put your ideas into writing that can be understood by others.

RULES FOR GOOD SPELLING

13a Develop basic spelling habits.

(1) Keep a list of troublesome words.

Write down the words that give you trouble in spelling. Make a list of each new word that you misspell or that you find hard to spell. Keep your list in a notebook. Then you can refer to it regularly.

When you think you have learned to spell a word on your list, put a check beside it. Try to check off all the words on the list.

(2) Study the hard parts of words.

See the Master Spelling List, pp. 284–286

Usually some part of a word is hard to spell. Do you remember that *recommend* has only one **c** and two **m**'s? Do you remember the silent letter in *wrist*?

Pick out the hard parts of words. Study those parts. Sometimes it helps to underline the troublesome letters. In the word *recommend,* you can underline the one **c** and the two **m**'s. In *wrist,* underline the **w**.

(3) See each syllable. Say each syllable. Write each syllable.

Attack words by syllables. A syllable is made up of one main vowel sound. It may have one or two consonant sounds with it, or it may have none.

EXAMPLES

LEATH-ER (leather)	This word has two syllables. Only the first syllable will cause you trouble in spelling. It is not spelled quite the way it sounds. Look hard at this syllable. Say it. Then write it.

CAF-E-TE-RI-A (cafeteria)	This word has five syllables. Only the first two might cause trouble. Look at each syllable in order. Say each one. Write each one.

(4) Use a dictionary.

Most dictionaries spell out each word by syllables. When you look up a word in the dictionary, be sure you start with the correct first letters.

See Sources of Information, pp. 288–296

13b Learn basic spelling rules.

Each spelling rule you learn can help you spell better. However, many rules have exceptions. So learn the exceptions to the rules also.

(1) Most nouns form their plurals by adding s or es.

EXAMPLES

Nouns that add **s**	train, train**s**
	shirt, shirt**s**
	apple, apple**s**
Nouns that add **es**	witch, witch**es**
	fox, fox**es**
	push, push**es**

Nouns that end in **ch, s, sh, x,** or **z** add **es** to form their plurals. Most other nouns add only **s.**

EXERCISE 1 Number a sheet of paper 1–9. Write the plurals of the following nouns.

EXAMPLE gas

gases

1. desk
2. box
3. pump
4. lass
5. wish
6. jet
7. hatch
8. birth
9. batch

(2) Nouns ending in *y* after a consonant change the *y* to *i* and add es to form the plural.

EXAMPLES berry, berr**ies**
penny, penn**ies**

If a vowel comes before the final **y**, just add **s**.

EXAMPLES pulley, pulley**s**
toy, toy**s**

EXERCISE 2 Number a sheet of paper 1–6. Next to each number, write the plural of the following nouns.

EXAMPLE pony

ponies

1. hobby
2. ferry
3. boy
4. monkey
5. surrey
6. baby

(3) Most nouns ending in *f* add *s* to form the plural.

EXAMPLE cliff, cliff**s**

(4) Some nouns ending in *f* or *fe* change the *f* to *v* and add es or *s*.

EXAMPLES wharf, wharves
wolf, wolves
wife, wives

(5) Most nouns ending in *o* following a vowel add *s* to form the plural.

EXAMPLES studio, studios
rodeo, rodeos

(6) Most nouns ending in *o* following a consonant add *es* to form the plural.

EXAMPLE tomato, tomatoes

(7) Most musical terms ending in *o* add only an *s* to form the plural.

EXAMPLES piano, pianos
soprano, sopranos

(8) Compound nouns usually form the plural on the most important part of the word.

EXAMPLES brother-in-law, brothers-in-law
vice-president, vice-presidents
football, footballs

(9) A few nouns are irregular and form their plurals without an *s* or an *es*. Some change spelling. Some remain the same.

EXAMPLES man, men
moose, moose
louse, lice

EXERCISE 3 Number a sheet of paper 1–20. Write the plural form of each of the following nouns. You may use a dictionary to check your work if you wish.

EXAMPLE dictionary

dictionaries

1. trio
2. woman
3. key
4. shelf
5. piano
6. belief
7. potato
8. alto
9. child
10. echo
11. chase
12. hiss
13. catch
14. cliff
15. hill
16. duty
17. mouse
18. radio
19. battery
20. father-in-law

Prefixes

A prefix is a syllable that can be added to the front of a word or the part of a word called the root to make a new word. An example is *un-* in the word *untie.* The prefix *un-* has been added to the root *tie* to make *untie. Untie* means the opposite of *tie.* Another prefix is *re-*. It makes *retie.* This means *tie again.*

Prefixes join to roots in this way. However, the spelling of the root remains the same, even when a prefix is added.

(10) A new word may be formed by adding a prefix to a root.

Most roots that add prefixes are words that can be used without the prefix. For example, the root *tie* may be used alone as a word. A few roots are not used without prefixes. For example, *receive* has the prefix *re-*. The root *ceive* cannot be used alone as a word.

Here are examples of prefixes, roots, and the new words they make.

PREFIX	ROOT	WORD
de-	-clare	declare
	-cline	decline
dis-	interest	disinterest
	appear	disappear
un-	armed	unarmed
	controlled	uncontrolled
in-	convenient	inconvenient
	-dividual	individual

EXERCISE 4 Number a sheet of paper 1–10. Next to each number, write the new word formed by adding the prefix to the root.

EXAMPLE dis + appoint

disappoint

1. de + cide
2. de + stroy
3. dis + appear
4. dis + satisfied
5. dis + solve
6. un + noticed
7. un + named
8. un + told
9. in + side
10. in + sane

EXERCISE 5 Number your paper 1–10. Next to each number write a word you make by combining a prefix with the root. Use the prefixes in the following list.

in-	dis-
im-	un-
non-	

EXAMPLE correct

incorrect

1. polite
2. human
3. may
4. complete
5. dependence
6. limited
7. made
8. agree
9. breakable
10. proper

When a prefix is added to a root, the spelling of the root remains the same. Sometimes the spelling of the prefix changes.

(11) Some prefixes change spelling when joined to a root.

The prefix *in-* becomes *im-*.

EXAMPLES

in-	mature	immature
in-	possible	impossible

The prefix *in-* becomes *il-*.

EXAMPLE

in-	legal	illegal

The prefix *in-* becomes *ir-*.

EXAMPLE

in-	-ritate	irritate

The prefix *com-* becomes *col-*.

EXAMPLE

com- -lect collect

The prefix *com-* becomes *con-*.

EXAMPLE

com- -nect connect

Suffixes

(12) A new word may be formed by adding a suffix to a word or root.

Sometimes a root adds letters at the end to make a new word. An example is *slow*. It adds *-ly* or *-ness*. These groups of letters are *suffixes*. The new words that are formed are *slowly* and *slowness*.

(13) Most words adding the suffixes *-ly* and *-ness* keep their same spelling.

EXAMPLES high, high**ly**
quick, quick**ness**
awful, awful**ly**

(14) Most words ending in *y* following a consonant change the *y* to *i* before adding a suffix that does not begin with *i*.

EXAMPLES merry, merr**ily**
jolly, joll**iness**
try, tr**ied**

Note: Names of people ending in **y** do not change spelling to show plural.

EXAMPLE The *Kellys* live here.

(15) Words or roots ending in *ie* usually change the *ie* to *y* when the suffix *-ing* is added.

EXAMPLES die, d**ying**
lie, l**ying**

(16) Most words ending in e omit the e when adding a suffix that begins with a vowel.

EXAMPLES face, fac**ing**
rise, ris**ing**

(17) Most words ending *-ce* or *-ge* keep the e when adding a suffix that begins with *a* or *o*.

EXAMPLES trace, trace**able**
courage, courage**ous**

(18) Most words ending in e keep the e when adding a suffix that begins with a consonant.

EXAMPLES manage, manage**ment**
base, base**ment**

(19) One-syllable words ending in a single consonant following a single vowel double the consonant when adding the suffixes *-ed*, *-ing*, or *-er*.

EXAMPLES tap, tap**ping**
rip, rip**ped**

EXERCISE 6 Following are words and suffixes. Number a sheet of paper 1–20. Next to each number, write the new word you make by joining the word and its suffix.

EXAMPLE icy + ly

icily

1. place + ing
2. natural + ly
3. drive + ing
4. crazy + ly
5. hurry + ing
6. sure + ness
7. sigh + ed
8. tie + ing
9. manage + able
10. encourage + ment
11. bake + ing
12. space + ing
13. lie + ing
14. play + ed
15. trip + ing
16. slap + ed
17. actual + ly
18. wrap + er
19. ordinary + ly
20. mighty + ly

SOUNDS OF LETTERS

Sometimes parts of different words have the same sound but different spellings. An example is *puff-rough.* These words rhyme, but their spellings are different.

In English, some sounds people make while speaking may be spelled several different ways.

13c Learn the different ways of spelling sounds.

A list of common sounds in English is given here. Next to each sound are examples of the various ways each sound is spelled in different words.

Sound	Examples
ch (as in *chair*)	**ch**air, wat**ch,** ques**t**ion, pic**t**ure
f (as in *fun*)	**f**un, pu**ff,** lau**gh, ph**one
g (as in *get*)	**g**et, **gh**ost
j (as in *judge*)	**j**udge, ma**g**ic, bri**dg**e, sol**d**ier
k (as in *kite*)	**k**ite, **c**at, **ch**oir, ba**ck**
m (as in *mat*)	**m**at, cli**mb,** ha**mm**ock, cal**m**
n (as in *not*)	**n**ot, **kn**ow, wi**nn**er, **gn**at, **pn**eumonia
sh (as in *shame*)	**sh**ame, mi**ss**ion, **s**ure, sta**t**ion, ma**ch**ine
t (as in *tell*)	**t**ell, walk**ed**
z (as in *zig-zag*)	**z**ig-**z**ag, doe**s,** sci**ss**ors
a (as in *ate*)	**a**te, **ai**d, br**ea**k
e (as in *be*)	b**e,** s**ee,** s**ea**t, p**eo**ple, rel**ie**f, rec**ei**ve, mach**i**ne, funn**y**
i (as in *pipe*)	p**i**pe, p**ie,** b**uy,** tr**y,** **eye**
i (as in *it*)	**i**t, b**ee**n, b**u**sy, b**ui**ld, w**o**men
o (as in *open*)	**o**pen, l**oa**d, t**oe,** b**ow**l, s**ew**
u (as in *united*)	**u**nited, b**eau**ty, p**ew,** **you**
u (as in rule)	r**u**le, s**ui**t, tr**oo**p, gr**ou**p, thr**ew,** m**o**ve

Homonyms

Homonyms are words that sound alike but are spelled differently. Their meanings are also very different. Some examples are *hear* and *here*. Misspellings can occur when you confuse homonyms.

13d Learn which spelling of a homonym belongs with the meaning you want.

HOMONYMS	MEANINGS
accept	to take what is given
except	leaving out; other than
affect	to change or to influence
effect	a result
already	earlier; in the past
all ready	(two words) completed; ready
capital	a city of government
capitol	the building of government
hear	to listen
here	in this spot
its	belonging to it
it's	it is (a contraction)
passed	went by (a verb)
past	of an earlier time
pair	two of anything
pare	to cut
pear	fruit
their	belonging to them
there	in that place
they're	they are (a contraction)

REVIEW EXERCISE A Missing Letters

Number a sheet of paper 1–10. Next to each number write the word with the missing letters. The number in parentheses tells you how many letters are missing from the word.

EXAMPLE an a__(2)__e in the head

ache

1. a good app__(1)__tite
2. the bru__(1)__se hurts
3. a strange bel__(2)__f
4. a decent buri__(1)__l
5. button the coll__(1)__r
6. remain con__(2)__ious
7. clever dec__(2)__t
8. tasty de__(2)__ert
9. deep gr__(2)__f
10. the h__(2)__ght of the tree

REVIEW EXERCISE B Plurals

Number a sheet of paper 1–10. Write the plural form of each of the following words. You may want to consult a dictionary.

EXAMPLE apple

apples

1. apology
2. belief
3. biography

4. calf
5. cemetery
6. elbow
7. chief
8. jealousy
9. obituary
10. paralysis

REVIEW EXERCISE C Syllables

Number a sheet of paper 1–10. On your paper divide each of the following words into syllables. The first one is done for you.

EXAMPLE accent

ac - cent

1. accent
2. bandage
3. biology
4. casualty
5. convalescent
6. descendant
7. skeleton
8. suicide
9. tantrum
10. vessel

REVIEW EXERCISE D Prefixes

Number a sheet of paper 1–15. Then add one of the following prefixes to each of the numbered words. Write the new words on your paper. You may want to consult a dictionary as you work.

in- non- im-
un- dis-

1. appetizing
2. breakable
3. belief
4. conscious
5. digestible
6. gratitude
7. hygienic
8. likable
9. natural
10. prejudiced
11. sincerely
12. sterilized
13. mature
14. stretched
15. appearance

REVIEW EXERCISE E Suffixes

Number a sheet of paper 1–15. Then add one of the following suffixes to each one of the numbered words. Write the words on your paper. You may want to consult a dictionary as you work.

-ing	-al
-ed	-ous
-ly	-ness

EXAMPLE swerve

swerving

1. ache
2. accent
3. chemical
4. serve
5. fatal
6. immature
7. intestine
8. nasal
9. scandal
10. sterilize
11. stingy
12. suicide
13. sweat
14. twinge
15. vague

REVIEW EXERCISE F Homonyms

Number a sheet of paper 1–15. After each number write the correct word from the parentheses.

EXAMPLE Sarah's dog can (here/hear) my whistle from a distance of two miles.

hear

1. As I (past/passed) my brother's room yesterday, I noticed that he had some old pictures spread on the floor.
2. (Its/It's) hard for me to resist those old pictures of our childhood.
3. (There/They're) sometimes embarrassing but always interesting.
4. Everyone in my family (accept/except) my brother enjoys these pictures.
5. I found one of my uncle when he first moved (here/hear) from his hometown.
6. He had (already/all ready) found a job and he looked quite happy.
7. Another picture was taken when my fourth grade class visited the (capitol/capital) of our state.
8. The whole class is standing on the steps of the (capitol/capital) building.
9. I was wearing a new (pair/pare/pear) of shoes which hurt my feet.
10. The (affect/effect) of my sore feet can be seen on my scowling little face.
11. I would not (accept/except) my family's advice that I wear some old, comfortable shoes instead of my new ones.
12. That field trip had a greater (affect/effect) on me than I expected.
13. Everyone in the fourth grade class who took the trip came home with sore throats (accept/except) the teacher.
14. (There/Their) she is in the picture, smiling as if she knew (already/all ready) that she would be the only healthy survivor of the trip.
15. These old photographs help me to remember and to enjoy the (past/passed).

MASTER SPELLING LIST

The following list includes words frequently misspelled. Your study of this list should be by groups of words. Practice spelling ten or twenty at a time. Be sure you also know the meaning of each word. Where necessary, look up words in a dictionary.

From time to time, review words you have misspelled at an earlier time. By doing this you help to keep their spellings clear in your mind.

The hard parts of words are printed in darker letters. The darkness of the letters will help you pay close attention to the parts often misspelled.

absen**c**e
a**cc**ident**all**y
a**cc**omp**any**
a**cc**ura**cy**
ach**ie**ve
a**c**quire
acro**ss**
a**ct**ually
administration
admi**tt**ance
advertis**e**ment
ag**ai**n
agricult**u**re
aisle
alt**ar**/alt**er**
amat**eur**
a**nn**ua**ll**y
apolo**g**y
a**pp**arent
a**pp**ear**a**nce
a**pp**rec**i**ate
a**pp**roach

a**pp**rov**al**
arg**ue**
arg**u**ment
a**rr**ang**e**ment
a**th**letic
a**tt**end**a**nce
auth**ori**ty
avail**a**ble

begi**nn**ing
behav**ior**
bel**ie**ve
benefit
benefited
breath (**e**)
bur**ie**d
bus**i**ness

calend**ar**
campai**g**n
capit**al**/capit**o**l
cemet**e**ry

certifi**c**ate
character
ch**ie**f
Christ**i**an
ch**oi**ce
ch**oo**se/ch**o**se
cloth**es**
col**o**r
col**umn**
co**mm**er**c**ial
co**mm**i**tt**ee
co**mm**unist
competit**o**r
complet**e**ly
con**c**entrate
confiden**t**ial
confu**si**on
con**sc**ience
con**sc**ious
contro**ll**ed
c**oo**perate
co**rr**espond**e**nce

courageous
criticism
criticize
cruelly
curiosity
curious
cylinder

deceive
decision
definite
dependent
describe
despair
desperate
difference
dining
dinner
disappearance
disappoint
discipline
doctor
duplicate

eager
easily
effect
eighth
eligible
embarrass
emphasize
encouragement
entirely
entrance
environment
equipped
especially
exaggerate
excellent
exciting
exercise
existence
expense
experiment
extremely

fantasy
fashionable
favorite
field
finally
financial
foreign
forty
forward
fourth
friend
further

genius
government
gracious
grammar
guarantee
guess
gymnasium

happened
happiness
hear/here
heavily
height
hopeless
hospital
humor
humorous
hungrily

ignorance
imagine
immediately
increase
individually
influence
ingredient
innocence
insurance
intelligence
interference
interrupt

jealous
judgment

knowledge

laboratory
laborer
laid
leisure
lessen/lesson
license
likely
listener
lively
loneliness
loose/lose/loss
luxury

magazine
maintenance
manufacturer
marriage
meant
mechanic
medical
medicine
merchandise
miniature
minimum
minute
mischief
mischievous

moral/morale
muscle
mysterious

naturally
niece
ninety
noticeable

obstacle
occasionally
occurrence
offensive
official
often
omission
omit
operate
opponent
opportunity
optimist
orchestra
organization
originally

paid
parallel
passed/past
peace/piece
peculiar
performance
permanent
personality
perspiration
persuade
physical
pleasant
politician
possession
practically
practice
preferred
prejudice
preparation
presence
pressure
privilege
probably
procedure
proceed
psychology
pursuit

quiet
quite

realize
receipt
recognize
recommend
referred
relieve
religious
removal
repetition
resistance
resource
responsibility
restaurant
rhythm
ridiculous

safety
satisfied
scarcity
scene
schedule
scholar
scissors
seize
separate
similar
simplify
sincerely
skiing
sophomore
specifically
sponsor
straight
strength
stretch
strictly
stubborn
substitute
succeed
successful
sufficient
summary
surprise
suspense
swimming

tendency
therefore
thorough
though
thoughtful
tragedy
transferred
truly

unanimous
unnecessary
useful
useless
usually

vacuum
valuable
various

weather/whether
weird
whole/hole

yield

CHAPTER

14

SOURCES OF INFORMATION

Finding out about the world can be fascinating when the facts you learn are interesting and useful. Before you can know and enjoy this information, you must know where to look for it.

This chapter tells you about the places where information is available. Knowing where to find information is an important part of your education.

The nearest place for information is your textbook, which you have open in front of you now.

TEXTBOOKS

Nearly all textbooks are divided into parts that make their information easy to find. Here are the parts of this textbook.

The *front cover* usually lists the title, the author, the publisher and the number of the book in the series. The *back edge* of the cover (called the "spine") often repeats that information and also gives the name of the publisher. Information on the spine identifies any book when several are stacked together.

The *inside cover* is also called the "end paper." In this book the inside back cover is used to show brief information about the history of the English language. Some books leave the end papers blank.

The *title page* repeats information from the cover and gives more information about the author and the publisher. The *copyright page* is usually the back of the title page. This page gives the date of publication and tells who owns the rights to the book. The *introduction* or *preface* explains what the book is about and how it can be used. It may also tell why certain features are included.

The *table of contents* lists chapter titles and contents by page numbers. The *text* contains the major contents of the book. The *index* is an alphabetic listing of the principal topics found in the text, with page numbers. The *glossary* defines many terms used in the book and often gives examples. Some books have no glossary. In some books the glossary is combined with the index.

THE DICTIONARY

As you know, words are very important in your life. A dictionary is a valuable source of information about words. Along with other information, a dictionary tells the meanings of words, how they are pronounced and spelled, and what parts of speech they are.

14a Learn to use the dictionary.

(1) Words are listed alphabetically.

Every dictionary alphabetizes words. Words that begin with *A* come first, followed by words that begin with *B,* then *C,* and so on through the alphabet.

Words beginning with the same letter are alphabetized by their second letters. *Able* comes before *across*. *Advance* comes after that. *Axe* and *azalea* come near the end of the *A* words.

Many words have the same first few letters. These words are alphabetized by the first letters that are different.

EXAMPLES limb
lime
limit
limp

EXERCISE 1 Number a sheet of paper 1–10. Write the following words in their correct alphabetical order.

saliva	sack
sail	scratch
saber	sand
scramble	shape
shack	scrape

(2) Guide words at the top of each page show which words are on that page.

There are two guide words at the top of every dictionary page that contains words. The first guide

aria 37 **armory**

A

a·ri·a [ä′rē·ə *or* âr′ē·ə] *n.* A song, usually in an opera or oratorio, sung by a single person to musical accompaniment.
ar·id [ar′id] *adj.* **1** Without enough rainfall to grow things; dry; parched. **2** Dull; dry: an *arid* speech. — **a·rid·i·ty** [ə·rid′ə·tē] *n.*
a·right [ə·rīt′] *adv.* Correctly; rightly: I don't remember *aright.*
a·rise [ə·rīz′] *v.* **a·rose, a·ris·en** [ə·riz′(ə)n], **a·ris·ing 1** To get up: He *arose* and began his speech. **2** To rise up; ascend: Wild duck *arose* from the lake. **3** To start; come into being: New problems always *arise.* **4** To result: The argument *arose* from her stubbornness.
ar·is·toc·ra·cy [ar′is·tok′rə·sē] *n., pl.* **ar·is·toc·ra·cies 1** A class of society inheriting by birth a high position or rank, certain powers and privileges, and usually wealth. **2** Government by this upper class. **3** Any group of those thought to be the best: an *aristocracy* of rich men.
a·ris·to·crat [ə·ris′tə·krat] *n.* **1** A member of an aristocracy; nobleman. **2** A person with the opinions, manners, or appearance of the upper class. **3** A person who prefers an aristocratic form of government.
a·ris·to·crat·ic [ə·ris′tə·krat′ik] *adj.* **1** Fit for an aristocrat; superior; exclusive; snobbish. **2** Belonging to, having the characteristics of, or favoring an aristocracy: *aristocratic* government. — **a·ris′to·crat′i·cal·ly** *adv.*
Ar·is·tot·le [ar′is·tot′(ə)l] *n.,* 384–322 B.C., famous Greek philosopher, a pupil of Plato.
a·rith·me·tic [ə·rith′mə·tik] *n.* The study of working with numbers, mainly in addition, subtraction, multiplication, and division.
ar·ith·met·i·cal [ar′ith·met′i·kəl] *adj.* Of or having to do with arithmetic.
ar·ith·met·ic progression [ar′ith·met′ik] A sequence of numbers such that the difference between any two successive numbers is the same, as 3, 7, 11, 15.
Ariz. Abbreviation of ARIZONA.
Ar·i·zo·na [ar′ə·zō′nə] *n.* A state in the sw U.S.
ark [ärk] *n.* **1** In the Bible, the ship Noah built to save himself, his family, and two of every kind of animal from the Flood. **2** A chest in the ancient Jewish Temple that held the stone … the Ten Commandments were … covenant.

ar·ma·da [är·mä′də] *n.* (*sometimes written* **Armada**) A fleet of warships: The Spanish *Armada* was defeated by the English in 1588. ◆ This word comes directly from a Spanish word, which in turn came from a Latin word meaning *armed.* It is closely related to the word *army.*
ar·ma·dil·lo [är′mə·dil′ō] *n., pl.* **ar·ma·dil·los** A small burrowing mammal found from South America north to Texas, having an armorlike shell of jointed plates. Some kinds can roll up, shell and all, into a ball when attacked.

Armadillo, about 28 in. long

ar·ma·ment [är′mə·mənt] *n.* **1** (*often pl.*) The military equipment, as guns, ships, bombs, used in war. **2** The armed forces of a nation, equipped for war.
ar·ma·ture [är′mə·choo͝r] *n.* **1** The rotating part of an electric motor or generator, having a soft-iron core surrounded by coils of insulated wire. **2** The part of an electric relay, buzzer, or bell, that is moved by the electromagnet.
arm·chair [ärm′châr′] *n.* A chair with supports on both sides for the arms or elbows.
armed forces [ärmd] All the military, naval, and air forces of a nation.
arm·ful [ärm′fo͝ol′] *n., pl.* **arm·fuls** As much as can be held by one or both arms.
arm·hole [ärm′hōl′] *n.* An opening for the arm in clothes.
ar·mi·stice [är′mə·stis] *n.* An agreement to stop fighting for a short time; truce.
Armistice Day The former name for VETERANS DAY.
ar·mor [är′mər] *n.* **1** A covering worn when fighting, to protect the body. **2** Any protective covering, as the shell of a turtle, or plates of a tank. ¶1
ar·mored [är′mərd] *adj.* **1** Protected by armor. **2** Equipped with tanks and other armored vehicles: an *armored* division. ¶1

word is the same as the first word on the page. The second guide word is the same as the last word on that page.

By looking at the guide words on a page, you can tell whether the word you want is listed there. For example, you may want to find the meaning of *amnesty.* You would turn to a page with the guide words *ammonia* and *amount.* How do you know *amnesty* is on that page?

The first two letters **am** are the same in all three words. The third letter in *amnesty* is **n**; **n** comes between **m** (the third letter in *ammonia*) and **o** (the third letter in *amount*). *Amnesty* is indeed on that page.

Also on that page will be the other words that have **amn** as the first three letters.

EXERCISE 2 Which of the following words would you find on a dictionary page with the guide words *endow* and *engine*? Write the words on a sheet of paper.

engage	English
enforce	endure
energy	engrave
enemy	engagement
endorse	enjoy

(3) Words are spelled by syllables.

See Syllable, p. 331

All entry words in most dictionaries are spelled out by syllables. *Adventure* is spelled out *ad-ven-ture,* for example. Suppose you do not know the whole spelling of a word. If you know the spelling of the first syllable, you have a good chance of finding the word in the dictionary.

> **a·rise** [ə·rīz′] *v.* **a·rose, a·ris·en** [ə·riz′(ə)n], **a·ris·ing 1** To get up: He *arose* and began his speech. **2** To rise up; ascend: Wild duck *arose* from the lake. **3** To start; come into being: New problems always *arise.* **4** To result: The argument *arose* from her stubbornness.

If you look for a word in one part of a dictionary and cannot find it, perhaps its spelling sounds one way but looks another way. Check the list of sounds and spelling in Chapter 13, p. 278, and try again.

EXERCISE 3 The following pairs of words contain one word spelled correctly and one spelled incorrectly. The first syllable of all words is correct. Number a sheet of paper 1–10. Write the correct spelling on your paper.

EXAMPLE per-son-al-i-ty
per-sen-al-i-ty

per-son-al-i-ty

1. foam-i-ness
   foam-y-ness
2. gal-ant-ry
   gal-lant-ry
3. hor-o-scope
   hor-i-scope
4. i-den-ti-cle
   i-den-ti-cal
5. lat-a-tude
   lat-i-tude
6. mag-nif-i-sent
   mag-nif-i-cent
7. mor-sil
   mor-sel
8. oc-a-sion
   oc-ca-sion
9. rum-ble
   rum-bel
10. ther-i-py
    ther-a-py

(4) The pronunciation of every word is given.

A dictionary uses a special marking system to show how to pronounce every word. The system of marks appears at the bottom of every other page in most dictionaries. The marks are called *diacritical marks*. They show what sound each part of a word has in speech. Most dictionaries also explain the pronunciation system in the front section. It will be helpful to you if you become familiar with the system in the dictionary you use.

(5) The part of speech is given for each word entry.

Usually a dictionary will give an abbreviation for the part of speech of every entry word. The abbreviation for *noun* is *n;* for *adjective* it is *adj.*

Some words can be used as more than one part of speech. Those words will have several abbreviations in a dictionary entry.

(6) Unusual plural spellings are given.

If a word that is a noun has an unusual plural spelling, the plural form is given. The abbreviation for plural is *pl.* This abbreviation is followed immediately by the spelling.

EXAMPLE *alumna* (pl. *alumnae*)

(7) Irregular verb forms are given.

Spellings are given for the simple past tense and the past participle of each irregular verb. For example, the entry word *sing* also has the forms *sang* and *sung* listed.

(8) Comparative and superlative forms are given for many adjectives and some adverbs.

You will find the comparative and superlative forms given for many adjectives. For example, *heavy* has the forms *heavier* and *heaviest* added.

Irregular adverbs also will have comparative and superlative forms listed. For example, the adverb *well* has the forms *better* and *best* added.

EXERCISE 4 On a sheet of paper write the plural form of the following nouns. You may check the forms in your dictionary.

EXAMPLE deer

deer

1. ox
2. daisy
3. fish
4. holiday
5. moose
6. mouse
7. bear
8. index

(9) Various meanings of words are given.

Dictionaries give different meanings for the words in them. Most words have more than one meaning.

EXAMPLE

seal (noun)
1. a printed design
2. something that closes or fastens
3. a stamp
4. a sea mammal

seal (verb)
1. to close up
2. to mark with a seal

The meaning you want depends upon how the word is used. The other words around the word tell you. These words are called the *context*.

EXAMPLE The seal swam away.
[You can tell *seal* is a noun with meaning #4 above: a sea mammal. That meaning fits correctly in the context of the sentence: *The sea mammal swam away.*]

In another sentence, *seal* will have a different meaning.

EXAMPLE Please seal the box.
[In this sentence you can tell by its position that *seal* is a verb. The sentence helps tell that *seal* means *close up.*]

EXAMPLE Please close the box.

EXERCISE 5 On a sheet of paper write the abbreviation used by your dictionary for the following parts of speech. After each abbreviation write an example.

EXAMPLE noun

n. puppet

1. adjective
2. conjunction
3. preposition
4. pronoun
5. verb
6. adverb

EXERCISE 6 On a sheet of paper write the simple past tense of the following verbs as given in your dictionary.

EXAMPLE win

won

1. ride
2. box
3. finger
4. singe
5. swing
6. burn
7. tie
8. bend

EXERCISE 7 On a sheet of paper write two different definitions from your dictionary for each of the following words.

EXAMPLE run

To move or go along by using steps that are faster than walking steps. The act of running

1. deck
2. blue
3. tag
4. can
5. head
6. case
7. branch
8. root
9. sail
10. stone

EXERCISE 8 Each of the words *round, back,* and *slip* has more than one meaning. One of these words belongs with each of the following definitions. Number a sheet of paper 1–8. Next to each number, write the word defined.

round *back* *slip*

1. to an earlier time
2. a fall
3. to support
4. shaped like a ring
5. an article of clothing
6. plump
7. a piece of paper
8. a period of time in a boxing match

THE LIBRARY

14b Learn how to use the sources of information in a library.

(1) The librarian.

A librarian knows what information the library has. Learn how the librarian can help you. However, learn for yourself the contents of your library. Use the librarian only for special help. You should become independent in finding and using the resources of your library.

(2) Books of fiction.

Fiction is the class of books whose stories are not true. Books of fiction are kept together in one section of every library. They are arranged alphabetically by the last names of the authors. For example, *Drums* by James Boyd will come before *Fifteen* by Beverly Cleary. Any book by Cleary will come before *Dorp Dead* by Julia Cunningham.

If the same author has several books in the fiction section, those books will be alphabetized by the first letters in the first main words of the titles. Three science fiction books by Andre Norton are *Moon of Three Rings, Victory of Janus,* and *Zero Stone.* They would be found in that order on the shelves.

(3) Books of nonfiction.

Nonfiction books are filled with all sorts of information. The information covers every subject anyone has thought about.

Organizing this information requires a system that is easy to understand and use. The Dewey decimal system meets this requirement. It is used in almost all American libraries. The Dewey decimal system has ten major divisions. Each division covers a broad subject. Each broad division has ten smaller divisions. Each smaller division is subdivided by ten again. Each major division is numbered, as is each subdivision.

THE DEWEY DECIMAL SYSTEM

BOOK NUMBERS	SUBJECTS
000–099	General works (reference materials such as encyclopedias)
100–199	Philosophy (the ideas people have about the meaning of life)
200–299	Religion (people's beliefs and faiths, including mythology)
300–399	Social sciences (government, the law, financial ideas, and others)
400–499	Language (dictionaries and other books about words and meanings)
500–599	Science
600–699	Technology (agriculture, aviation, engineering, and others)
700–799	The Arts (art, architecture, dance, painting, music, and others)
800–899	Literature (plays, television scripts, poetry, and books about literature
900–999	History (information about the past, biographies, and travel books)

Thousands of new books are published every year. Every nonfiction book receives a Dewey decimal number. With these numbers, a library can keep its nonfiction books organized.

For example, a new book about mythology will be given a number in the 200–299 range. A new dictionary will have a number in the 400–499 range.

EXERCISE 9 On a sheet of paper write the Dewey decimal number range for each of the following.

EXAMPLE *Fishes of the World*

500-599

1. *Best Plays of 1977–1978*
2. *Flight and Flying*
3. *Beliefs and Religion*
4. a book about the origin of cats
5. *Jefferson of Monticello*
6. *Bicycle Motocross*
7. a book about myths of the ancient Egyptians
8. *The Times Atlas of the World*
9. *The Story of Art*
10. *General Principles of Language*

(4) The card catalog.

A set of small cabinet drawers containing cards is available in every library. Information is printed on the cards about the books in the library. All the books—fiction and nonfiction—have cards.

Fiction books have two cards. One is an *author card.* It is alphabetized by the author's last name.

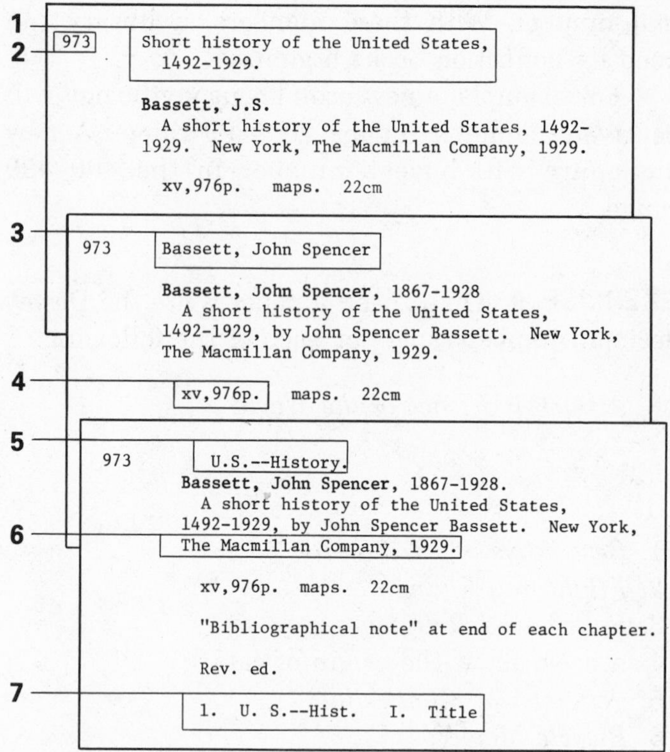

1 Title heading
2 Call number
3 Author
4 Book's physical description
5 Subject heading
6 Publisher, publication date
7 Other headings under which the book is listed

The other is a *title card.* It is alphabetized by the first main word in the title.

Nonfiction books have three cards each: the *author card,* the *title card,* and the *subject card.* All these cards are alphabetized. If you know either the subject or the author you can find out if the book is available.

You may want to find a new book about a subject, such as sea diving. By looking in the subject card catalog, you can find out if a book about this subject is in the library. Cards for books about exploring the sea will be under *S* in the subject catalog.

EXERCISE 10 Use the card catalog in a library to find a nonfiction book about three of the following subjects. For each book, write the Dewey decimal number, the title, the author, the date of publication, and the number of pages.

1. Tropical fish
2. Soccer
3. Nuclear power
4. Motorcycles
5. Ballet
6. Clothing styles

(5) Reference works.

Encyclopedias offer general information about most subjects. Usually the subjects will be arranged in alphabetical order. Each subject treated is printed in large letters of dark type. Following the names of subjects comes the information about the subject.

Suppose you want to look up information in an encyclopedia about *dogs*. Under that heading you will find out about kinds of dogs, what use they are to people, and how dogs are trained. An encyclopedia might tell you about their care and feeding. There may be references to other books that give special information about dogs.

Pictures often accompany the articles about subjects. Charts or graphs may also be included.

Atlases are books of geography. They contain maps. These maps may show all parts of the world or special sections. Some atlases give detailed information about population, climate, natural resources, and scientific facts.

Almanacs give facts about special subjects. Some of these subjects are as follows:

sports records
important events of the year
population figures
weather information
financial figures

Almanacs are usually published once each year. This makes it possible for them to offer up-to-date information.

(6) Periodicals.

Periodicals are materials printed regularly over short periods of time. (The word *periodical* is related to periods of time.) Some periodicals are published daily. Some come out every month. Most periodicals are magazines.

The most popular periodical magazines are listed in one place. This is the *Readers' Guide to Periodical Literature.* Its short name is the *Readers' Guide.*

The *Readers' Guide* publishes twenty-two issues a year. In it you can find information about the articles and stories published in more than one hundred leading periodicals in the United States.

A sample of part of a page is shown here.

SPACE programs. See Space research
SPACE research
Space sciences (cont) Sci N 111:58, 72, 106, 185, 267 Ja 22-29, F 12, Mr 19, Ap 23, '77

International aspects

See also
United Nations—Committee on the Peaceful Uses of Outer Space

United States

Ambitious new goals for U.S. space program. il U.S. News 82:98-9 My 9 '77
SPACE shuttle simulators. See Space flight simulators

EXERCISE 11 On a sheet of paper write the following information.

1. The titles of two magazine articles about the test flights of the United States space shuttle in the summer of 1977.
2. The names and dates of the magazines that published the articles.
3. The title of a more recent magazine about the United States space shuttle, with the name and date of the magazine.

(7) Audiovisual materials.

Some libraries have audio-visual materials. Sound recordings on records or cassettes may be listened to with earphones. A few libraries have filmstrips or even motion picture films.

Your librarian will be able to tell you what audio-visual materials are available in your library.

A BASIC LIST OF CONTENTS OF THE LIBRARY

Almanacs: Yearly calendars of facts and events, especially ones in nature such as weather predictions and the first day of spring.

Atlases: Books of maps, often with written information about places shown on the maps.

Audiovisual materials: Audio recordings on disks, tapes, or cassettes; filmstrips; motion picture films; microfilms; video recordings.

Bibliographies: Lists of books, usually alphabetized by titles, by authors, or by subjects, including information about publishers. An *annotated bibliography* includes comments about the contents of the listed books.

Books

Fiction: Novels and long or short stories made up by authors.

Nonfiction: Autobiographies, biographies, accounts of instruction such as cookbooks.

Collected works: Plays, poems, songs, musical pieces, scripts of television or other shows, art reproductions, and photographs.

Dictionaries: Alphabetical listings of words and names with definitions, pronunciations, and related information.

Encyclopedias: Books containing general information about people, places, and things known to people, alphabetically arranged.

Indexes: Alphabetical listings of topics, names, or other subject matter.

Pamphlets: Loosely bound, paper-covered sets of printed sheets containing nonfiction information.

Periodicals: Magazines or journals published regularly such as once a week or every month.

OTHER SOURCES OF INFORMATION

14c Learn to use other sources of information

People who are experts on a variety of topics probably live in your community. Sometimes it is better to find a local expert on a topic rather than to depend just on library information.

Local officials and authorities can provide facts that you may find important. For example, what special laws does your community have for teenagers? Are there laws that allow you special priv-

1. My dentist gives her patients *gas* when she drills a painful place.
2. Some of the men *gassed* in World War I are still in veterans' hospitals.
3. The bank robbers were caught when they ran out of *gas* on the freeway.
4. Canaries were used in coal mines to detect the presence of dangerous *gases*.
5. Call the utility company if *gas* is escaping from your stove.

2. **face** (fās)—*n.* **1.** the front part of the head. **2.** confidence or boldness. **3.** dignity or prestige. **4.** the surface of anything, esp. the front. **5.** the main or surface side of anything. **6.** in print, the style of printing type.
—*v.t.* **faced** (fāst) **1.** to confront boldly. **2.** to meet face to face.

A. What is the past tense of the verb *to face*?
B. How many meanings does the dictionary list for *face* used as a noun?
C. Number a sheet of paper 1–5. Write the number of the dictionary definition that matches the meaning of the word as it is used in each sentence.

1. Your *face* needs some soap and water.
2. We have *faced* our enemy and defeated him.
3. I want an architect to redesign the *face* of the building.
4. You look as if you cannot *face* another peanut butter sandwich.
5. Caroline made an embarrassing mistake last week, but she saved *face* with her perfect paper today.

REVIEW EXERCISE D Fiction

Number a sheet of paper 1–10. List the following novels (fiction books) in the order in which you would find them on the fiction shelves of a library.

1. *The Hobbit* by J. R. Tolkien
2. *The Pearl* by John Steinbeck
3. *The Grapes of Wrath* by John Steinbeck
4. *Lord of the Rings* by J. R. Tolkien
5. *The Sword in the Stone* by T. H. White
6. *Old Yeller* by Fred Gipson
7. *The Sea Wolf* by Jack London
8. *The Call of the Wild* by Jack London
9. *Big Red* by Jim Kjelgaard
10. *Fifth Chinese Daughter* by Jade Snow Wong

REVIEW EXERCISE E Card Catalog

Read carefully the following sample card from the card catalog. Number a sheet of paper 1–8. Answer each of the questions about the card.

```
506.9   Jacoby, John


            Careers and opportunities in science;
        a survey of all fields; with an introduction
        by Judith Jones.


        194 p.  illus.

        1.  Science as a profession
        2.  Title
```

1. What is the title of the book?
2. What is the name of the author?
3. What is the call number of the book?
4. Why is the book listed in the 500 section of the library's division by the Dewey decimal system?
5. How many pages long is the book?
6. Would the book help you learn about a career in chemistry? How do you know?
7. Under what other headings is this book listed in the card catalog?
8. Under what letter of the alphabet would you find this card in the card catalog?

REVIEW EXERCISE F **The Whole Library**

Look again at the review of materials available in a library on pages 303–304 in the textbook. Number a sheet of paper 1–10. After each number tell to what source you might first go in a library to find the answer to the question.

EXAMPLE What is the highest mountain in North America?
atlases or almanacs

1. What is the plural form of the word *cherub*?
2. Where was Abraham Lincoln born?
3. How might you go about making mayonnaise?
4. What is the capital of North Dakota?
5. What is the correct pronunciation of *prestigious*?
6. How many baseball games did the Cincinnati Reds win in 1976?

7. Who was Frank Lloyd Wright?
8. What countries border on Ethiopia?
9. Did any magazines review the film *King Kong* when it first appeared in May, 1976?
10. What is the body temperature of a cobra?

GLOSSARY

This glossary lists special terms that appear in the text. Most terms are defined here. Terms not defined are cross-referenced to other terms with definitions. Wherever examples will help, they are provided.

References to parts of the text appear with many terms in this glossary. The text treats these terms more fully.

Adjective A word that describes a noun. See **1g**.

The *blue* pencil broke.

She dropped it from *nervous* fingers.

An adjective helps *compare things*. Most adjectives change form to show comparison.

Kelly is a *tall* midget.

I've never seen a *taller* midget.

He is probably the *tallest* midget in the world.

Adverb A word that *describes* sentence *actions*. An adverb tells *where, when,* or *how* something happens. It usually does this by describing the verb in the sentence. An adverb can also describe some other part of speech. See **2c**.

These adverbs tell *where* the action happens.

We stayed *uptown.*

Here we are.

These adverbs tell *when* the action happens.

She arrived *early.*

She will leave *tomorrow.*

These adverbs tell *how* the action happens.

Ada ate *carefully.*

The bus *slowly* rolled away.

Agreement The forms of words that show the same number.

One *candy tastes* good.
Two *candies taste* better.

When you have *three candies, they* make you sick sometimes.

Antecedent The word or group of words referred to by a following pronoun.

The *person who* waits too long misses an opportunity.

Antonym A word that means the opposite of another word.

fat/thin, high/low, hot/cold, sad/happy

Apostrophe A mark that looks like a comma above the line to show possession, missing letters, or the plural of numbers. See **11g(1)–(3), 11h**.

Walt's shoe, won't, 6's

Appositive A word or group of words placed next to another to explain a meaning or idea.

He cut his cuticle, *the skin next to the nail.*
Marv, *a strong hiker,* walked fourteen miles.

Article The words *a, an,* and *the.* An article is a kind of adjective.

Auxiliary verb (See **Helping verb.**)

Case The form of a pronoun that shows its relation to other parts of the sentence. See **1e(1)–(3)**

SUBJECTIVE CASE usually serves as the subject of a sentence.

She rides.

POSSESSIVE CASE shows ownership.

Her friend rides.

OBJECTIVE CASE usually serves as the object of the sentence or the object of a preposition.

Follow *her.*
Stay near *her.*

Clause A group of words with both a subject and a predicate. A clause can be a sentence or part of a sentence. See **4c(1)** and **(2)**.

INDEPENDENT CLAUSE A clause that can stand alone as a complete thought.

The water froze and *the people shivered.* [two clauses in one sentence]
The water froze. The people shivered. [separate sentences]

DEPENDENT CLAUSE A clause that depends upon an independent clause to complete its thought.

When the water froze, the people shivered.

A dependent clause can work like a noun, an adjective, or an adverb in a sentence.

Colloquial Acceptable words or forms in informal conversation, but usually not acceptable in formal speech or writing.

They made money *hand over fist.*
Why does she *hang around* so much?

Comparison The forms of an adjective or adverb that show more or less about the words they describe. (See also **Modifiers.**)

POSITIVE *happy, bad*

COMPARATIVE *happier, worse*

SUPERLATIVE *happiest, worst*

Completer A word or words that complete a statement about the subject of a sentence. A completer comes after the verb. It is part of the predicate. (See also **Predicate.**) See **4f**.

Completers are words or phrases that can fit in sentence blanks like these:

Amy bit ______.
She felt ______.

NOUNS AND NOUN WORD GROUP COMPLETERS
Amy bit *the candy bar.*
She felt *the nut.*

ADJECTIVE COMPLETER
She is *young*.

ADVERB COMPLETER
She is *here*.

Complex sentence A sentence with an independent clause and a dependent clause. (See also **Clause.**) See **4c(4)**.

She went to school although she was sick. [*She went to school* is the independent clause; *although she was sick* is the dependent clause.]

Compound A word or group of words made up of two or more parts that could stand alone.

COMPOUND WORD *salesperson, football*

COMPOUND SUBJECT *Cats* and *dogs* may enter the contest.

COMPOUND OBJECT They want a fried *egg* and some *toast*.

COMPOUND PREDICATE Schools of fish *swim together* and *look for food*.

Compound sentence A sentence made up of two or more independent clauses. See **4c(3)**.

Shecky Masters makes surfboards, but he can't ride them.

Compound verb Two or more verbs in a clause or sentence. See **4b(4)**.

Jerry Tate *whistled* and *sang* the tune.

Conjunction A word that connects words, phrases, or clauses. Two kinds of conjunctions are *coordinating conjunctions* and *subordinating conjunctions*. See **2f**.

> COORDINATING CONJUNCTIONS connect parts of words, phrases, or clauses. The most common coordinating conjunctions are *and, but,* and *or.*
>
> eggs *and* bacon
> Wally tries *but* he always loses.
>
> SUBORDINATING CONJUNCTIONS connect ideas not equal to each other. Some examples are *after, although, as, because, before, like, since, though, unless, until, when, where, while.*
>
> We can sleep *until* the alarm rings.
> She changed the tire *because* it was flat.

Consonants All alphabet letters that are not vowels (**b, c, d,** for example). Consonant sounds are made in speaking by closing or bringing together parts of the throat, mouth, teeth, tongue, or lips.

Contractions A word form using an apostrophe to show missing letters.

> *can't, don't, could've*

Dangling modifier A modifying word or word group without a subject to modify.

> *While trying to swallow,* the piece of food got stuck in her throat.
> [This sentence seems to say the piece of food was trying to swallow!]

CORRECTED *While trying to swallow,* she got a piece of food stuck in her throat.

Dependent clause (See **Clause.**)

Determiner (See also **Article.**) Determiners are words like *a, an, the, one, some, their.* A determiner is a kind of adjective that always is followed by a noun.

a cloud, *a* young tree

the tired old dog, *an* old dog

Determiners help tell whether a noun is singular or plural.

a dog, *two* pens, *some* horses

Diacritical marks Marks used with letters to show how they are pronounced.

Examples are **ā** [as in *say*], **ĕ** [as in *set*], **ä** [as in *father*].

Diagraming A way of showing how parts of a sentence relate to one another. Two main types of diagraming are sometimes used. One type is a traditional diagram. The other is a tree diagram.

Any diagram of a sentence is only one way of showing the relationships among parts of a sentence.

TRADITIONAL DIAGRAMING Six sentences are diagramed below. Each diagram shows how added parts of a sentence fit together.

(1) The horse ate the hay.

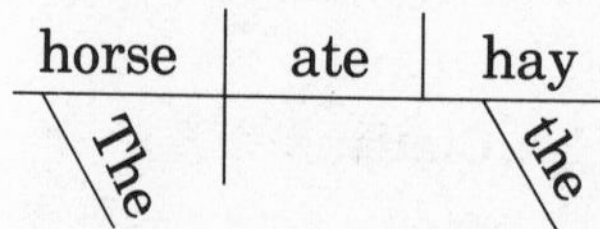

[The simple subject belongs first on the horizontal line. Under it on a slanted line belongs its modifier. The verb follows the simple subject, separated by a vertical line through the horizontal line. The direct object follows the verb, separated by a vertical line resting on the horizontal line.]

(2) The old horse ate the hay.

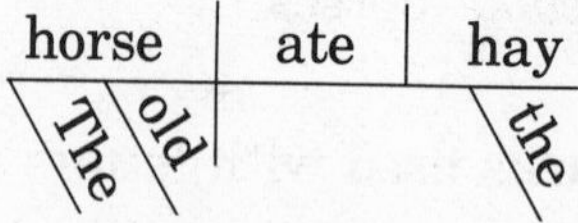

[Additional modifiers of the subject belong on additional slanted lines.]

(3) The old horse in the stall ate the hay.

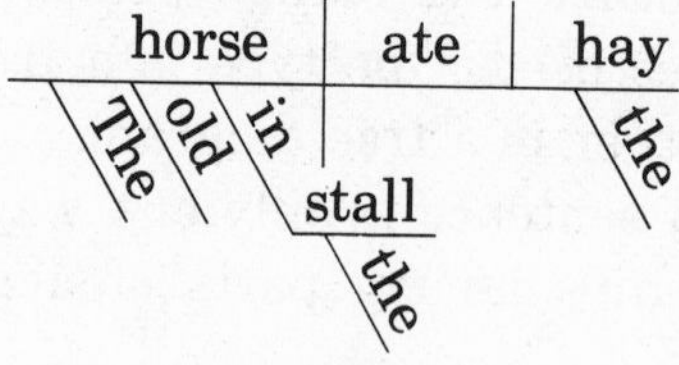

[A prepositional phrase modifying the subject belongs on slanted and horizontal lines as shown in (3) above.]

(4) The horse had eaten the hay.

horse | had eaten | hay
The
the

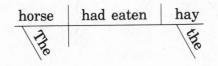

[Helping verbs belong with the main verb on the horizontal line.]

(5) The horse ate the hay slowly.

horse | ate | hay
The
slowly
the

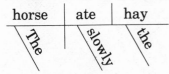

[An adverb belongs on a slanted line under the verb it modifies.]

(6) The old horse in the stall had eaten the new hay slowly.

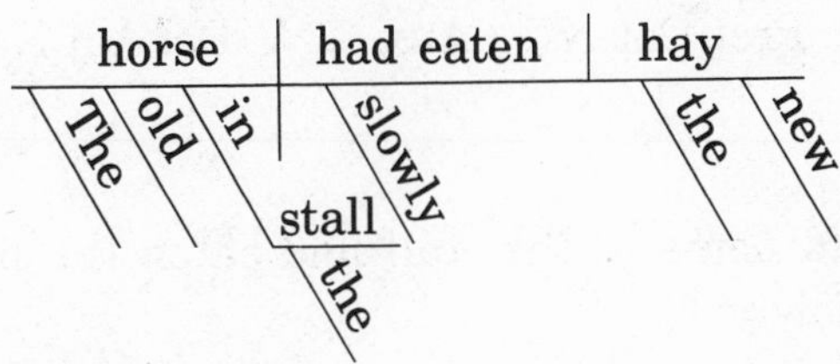

[The completed diagram is shown in (6) above.]

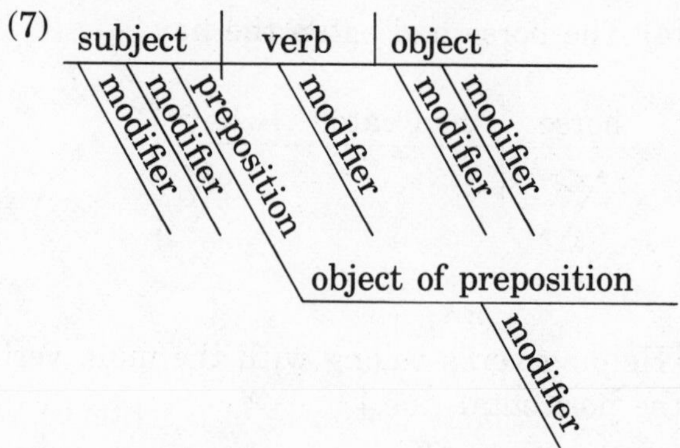

[All parts of the sentence are shown in (7) above.]

TREE DIAGRAMING

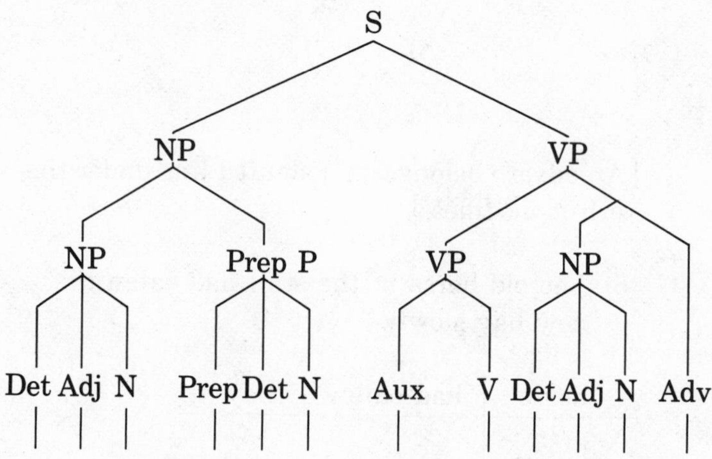

The old horse in the stall had eaten the new hay slowly.

A tree diagram gets its name from its shape. Turn it upside down and it looks a little bit like a tree. The abbreviations used in the tree diagram have the following meanings. These meanings are not all the same as those in traditional grammar. Follow your teacher's direction in using these meanings.

S: Sentence
NP: Noun phrase [A noun phrase is often the complete subject or the object of a sentence. It may have another, smaller phrase in it.]
VP: Verb phrase [A verb phrase can be the complete predicate of a sentence. It can have a verb phrase and a noun phrase in it.]
Prep P: Prepositional phrase
Det: Determiner
Adj: Adjective
N: Noun
Prep: Preposition
Aux: Auxiliary [a helping verb]
V: Verb
Adv: Adverb

Double Negative The incorrect use of two words that mean "no" in the same sentence. The most common negatives are *no* and *not*. Other negatives are *none (no + one)*, *nothing (no + thing)*, *never (not + ever)*, and *neither (not + either)*.

Here are examples of double negatives:

1. I do*n't* have *none*.
2. I did*n't* say *nothing*.

Here are two ways to correct each sentence:

1. I don't have one. (or any) [Remove second negative.]
   I have none. [Remove first negative.]

2. I didn't say a thing. (or anything) [Remove second negative.]
   I said nothing. [Remove the first negative. Change *say* to *said* so it will mean the same thing as *did say.*]

Expletive The word *it* or *there* when used as a filler to start a sentence.

> *It* is going to snow.
> *There* were some clouds in the sky.

Exposition Writing that expresses, explains, or "exposes" one's ideas, for example, a newspaper editorial, an essay, or a research paper.

Fragment An incomplete sentence, one without either the necessary subject or predicate. See **4g**.

> Running on the sand. [Who or what is running?]
>
> CORRECTED The bulls came running on the sand.

Helping verb Words that are used with verbs. The most common helping verbs are listed here. See **2a(3)**.

> am, are, is, was, were, being, been
> do, does, did, done
> have, has, had

Here are some other common helping verbs:

> can, could, may, shall
> will, would, might

Helping verbs help the verbs express their actions.

> Nan *is* running fast these days.
> Tami *did* run in the race Saturday.
> She *may* run next week.
> He *would* run.

Helping verbs also help show time.

> He *will* work tonight. [action in the future]
> She *has* worked a full day. [action completed in the past]

Idiom A word or phrase used in a special way.

> She *did herself proud.*

Independent clause A group of words having a subject and predicate able to stand by itself without need of other words to finish its meaning. [See also **Clause.**] See 4c(1).

Indirect object The secondary receiver of sentence action.

> She gave *him* a present. [To whom did she give it? Answer: *him.*]

Infinitive The standard or base form of a verb, often with *to.*

> to live, to eat

The infinitive is sometimes used as a noun.

> *To eat* is a necessity.

Inflection The change in the form of a word to show a change in meaning or grammatical use.

dog [singular], *dogs* [plural], *dogs'* [plural possessive]
sing [present], sang [past], sung [past participle]

Interjection A part of speech showing strong feeling. An interjection is not grammatically related to the sentence. See **2g**.

"*Tarnation!*" is all he could say.

Irregular verb A verb that does not add **ed** to form the past tense. (See also **Verb.**) See **2b(2)**.

Italics Slanted letters printed to draw special attention.

Linking verb A verb that links the subject to the subject completer. See **2a(2)**.

appear, become, feel, look, and forms of the verb *be*

Main clause An independent clause.

Metaphor A figure of speech in which one item is compared to another.

Her hair was *a mop.*

Modal auxiliary A verb used as a verb helper that does not change form.

can, could, might, ought

Modifiers Words used to describe someone, something, or some action. [See also **Adjective** and **Adverb.**]

Mood The purpose of the speaker as shown in the form and use of the verb. The three moods are (1) to state something, (2) to order or request something, and (3) to show a condition that is not true or is desirable.

(1) INDICATIVE MOOD They *own* a car.

(2) IMPERATIVE MOOD Step down, please.

(3) SUBJUNCTIVE MOOD They wish you *were* quieter.

Nominative The subjective case. (See also **Case.**)

Nonrestrictive clause or phrase A group of words that tells something more about someone or something in the same sentence. A nonrestrictive clause or phrase is not necessary to make the sentence complete, but it adds to its meaning.

> The mountain road, *muddy and rutted,* was a dangerous route. [phrase]
> The mountain road, *which was muddy and rutted from the rains,* was a dangerous route. [clause]

Noun A word or group of words that names a *person, place, thing,* or *idea.* See **1a**.

> Names of persons: Tim Eller, Jane McGuire, Scotty Campbell [proper nouns]
> Names of places: Sydney, Union Square, Uranus [proper nouns]
> Names of things: fog, trees, rocks [common nouns]
> Names of ideas: liberty, hope, weariness [common nouns]

Number One or more than one person or thing. In English, singular or plural number is shown in most nouns by the addition of **s** or **es**.

pin/pin**s**, glass/glass**es**

A few nouns change their spellings in special ways.

man/men, ox/oxen, goose/geese

Number is shown in most pronouns by a change in form.

this/these that/those
he, she/they her, him/them
hers, his/theirs

Object The result of action or the receiver of the action in a sentence. See **4e**.

DIRECT OBJECT He wants his *money.*

INDIRECT OBJECT The bank gave *him* his money.

The object of a preposition is a noun or pronoun which is related to another word by the preposition.

Give the money to *him*.

Objective case Pronouns show the objective case when they serve as the objects of a sentence or of a preposition. (See also **Case.**)

Alice introduced *him* to *her.* [*Him* and *her* are in the objective case.]

Paragraph A paragraph is a group of sentences beginning with an indention. The sentences should all be about one idea. There should be enough sentences to make the idea clear to the reader. See **5a–5c**.

The topic of a paragraph is often written in a topic sentence. The topic sentence usually comes at the beginning of a paragraph.

> *The types of household electrical appliances sold today would amaze our great grandparents.* Ten-speed blenders stir up any kind of food. Can openers cut open metal tops with ease. Crushed ice drops from a refrigerator door. A small cabinet cooks food in minutes by radiation. These and other gadgets perform miracles never dreamed of a few decades ago.

Participle The **ing** or the **ed** form of a verb that can be used as an adjective. A few irregular verbs form their participles in irregular ways. (See also **Phrase.**)

> happening [present participle]
> happened [past participle]
> broken [past participle of irregular verb *break*]

Parts of speech English sentences can have eight main kinds of words in them. These eight kinds of words are called parts of speech. These words do the work of the sentence. They help show meaning.

The eight parts of speech are *noun, pronoun, verb, adjective, adverb, preposition, conjunction*, and *interjection*. (See separate listings.)

Phrase A group of words belonging together, but not making a complete statement. See 3a.

PREPOSITIONAL PHRASE under the box

VERB PHRASE having started

NOUN PHRASE a terrible storm

Plural More than one. The plural is shown by words that mean more than one *(many, ten)*. It is also shown in the forms of nouns *(man/men)*, pronouns *(her/them)*, and verbs (she *runs*/they *run*).

Possessive A form of a noun or pronoun showing that someone owns something or that things belong close together.

the *girl's* slipper [possessive noun]
his plan [possessive pronoun]

Predicate The part of a sentence that tells about the subject. See 4b(2).

Charlie (S) pounded the nails into the shingles (P).

The bobcat (S) grabbed the meat and ran up the tree (P).

PREDICATE ADJECTIVE (See **Completer.**)

PREDICATE NOUN (See **Completer.**)

Prefix A prefix is one or more syllables added to the front of a word or root to affect its meaning. See 13b(10)–(11).

ungrateful, **pre**pay, **under**line, **dis**trust, **sub**way, **co**pilot, **in**direct, **non**payment

Preposition A part of speech that points out how two words are related. Most prepositions show time or place or direction. See 2e.

in a while, *of* the house, *before* the class.

Prepositional phrase (See **Phrase.**)

Pronoun A word that can stand for a noun. Usually, a pronoun stands for a group of words in which the noun is the main word. See 1e.

The silly little kitten raced into the room. *It* raced into the room. [*It* stands for the group of words.]

The truck with the red cab passed them.
It passed them.

That was *Cliff Anderson's* truck.
That was *his* truck.

Three cases of pronouns are found above. The first is the *subjective case.* It usually shows the doer of the action in a sentence.

It raced into the room.
It passed them.

The second case of the pronoun is the *objective case.*

It passed *them.*

The third case of the pronoun is the *possessive case.*

That was *his* truck.
We're waiting for Marge's call. We're waiting for *her* call.

Punctuation The marks used with words to show how they relate and how they are to be read. See Chapters 10–11.

Root The basic part of a word. Parts are added to it to change its meaning. (See also **Prefix** and **Suffix**.)

dis*trust*, re*play*, *play*able

Run-on sentence Two or more sentences run together without correct punctuation or connecting words. See **4h**.

Cheryl kept on talking from the stage the audience grew more and more restless.

Sentence A group of related words needing no other words to complete its thought. A sentence has a *subject* and a *predicate*. See **4a**.

SENTENCE The audience was ready to get up and leave.

NONSENTENCE Ready to get up and leave. (See also **Fragment**.)

Singular Only one of anything. (See **Plural** for a comparison.)

Slang A word or phrase not yet accepted for general use by most educated people.

He's a *laid-back dude*.
Far out!

Subject A noun (or its equal) that the rest of its sentence says or asks something about. The subject of a sentence is the *who* or *what* that belongs with the predicate. See **4b(1)**.

Deanna played the cello.
Asia is a huge continent.

Subject completer (See **Completer.**)

Subordinate clause A dependent clause. (See also **Clause.**)

Subordinating conjunction (See **Conjunction.**)

Suffix One or more syllables that add meaning to a word or root. A suffix is added to the end of a word or a root. See **13b(12).**

agree**ment,** sad**ly,** slow**er,** tall**est,** squeam**ish,** tact**ful,** nin**th,** flex**ible**

Syllable A letter or group of letters containing a vowel that is pronounced as one unit. A syllable may be a single vowel.

i-so-late, e-ject, a-ble

Most syllables contain a vowel sound plus a consonant sound or sounds.

de-mand, re-veal, se-cret [2 syllables]
un-hap-py, in-sur-ance, re-place-ment [3 syllables]
un-re-ward-ed, re-place-a-ble [4 syllables]

Synonym A word that means the same as another.

fall/autumn
tired/weary
clear/transparent

Syntax The arrangement of words and parts of a sentence.

The coach gave them a pep talk.
The coach gave a pep talk to them.
They were given a pep talk by the coach.

Tense Time as shown by the form of a verb. See **2b**.

PRESENT you *swim,* he *swims*

PAST you *swam,* she *swam*

FUTURE you *will swim,* they *are going to swim*

Topic sentence (See **Paragraph.**)

Transformation The changes in form that can be made in sentences and word groups.

Unity In composition, making sentences refer to the same topic or subject.

Verb A part of speech that shows action *(run),* states something *(is),* or shows condition *(seems).* Most verbs change their form to show time *(run—ran).* (See **Tense.**) Other changes show number (One woman *was* there. More *were* not.). See **2a**.

A verb tells the action in a sentence. Or it tells that something exists. Exists means "is" or "to be."

action: falls, shouts, groans
exists: is, are, am, was, were

Verbal A form of a verb used as another part of speech. (See **Infinitive.**)

Vocabulary The words and their meanings used in a language.

Voice The form of a verb that shows who or what is doing something.

ACTIVE VOICE The wind *blew* the curtain.

PASSIVE VOICE The curtain *was blown* by the wind.

Vowel The letters **a, e, i, o, u** and sometimes the letters **y** and **w.**

INDEX

A

B

C

D

F

G

H

I

J

L

M

P

Q

R

S

T

X

Y

Z

TAB KEY INDEX

CORRECTION SYMBOL	DEFINITION	CHAPTER
ad	adjectives and adverbs	7
adj	adjective	1
adv	adverb	2
agr	agreement of subjects and verbs	7
ap	apostrophe	11
cap	capital letter	9
cl	clause	4
comp	incomplete or false comparison	5
conj	conjunction	2
cxt	context	2
dm	dangling or misplaced modifier	
dn	double negative	7
frag	fragment	4
g	good use	
glos	glossary	
info	sources of information	14
inj	interjection	2
ital	italics	11
k	awkward sentence	
let	letter writing	6
n	noun	1
nc	not clear	
p	error in punctuation	
paral	parallelism	
phr	phrase	3

TAB KEY INDEX
(Continued)

CORRECTION SYMBOL	DEFINITION	CHAPTER
plan	planning and writing a composition	6
prep	preposition	2
pro	pronoun	1
ref	reference of pronouns	7
ro	run-on sentence	4
sp	spelling	13
spk	speaking and listening	12
ss	sentence structure	4
verb	verb	2
ww	wrong word	8
¶	paragraph	5
./	period	10
?	question mark	10
!	exclamation mark	10
,/	comma	10
;/	semicolon	11
:/	colon	11
-/	hyphen	11
”/	quotation marks	11
( )	parentheses	11
[ ]	brackets	
—	dash	

B 9
C 0
D 1
E 2
F 3
G 4
H 5
I 6
J 7

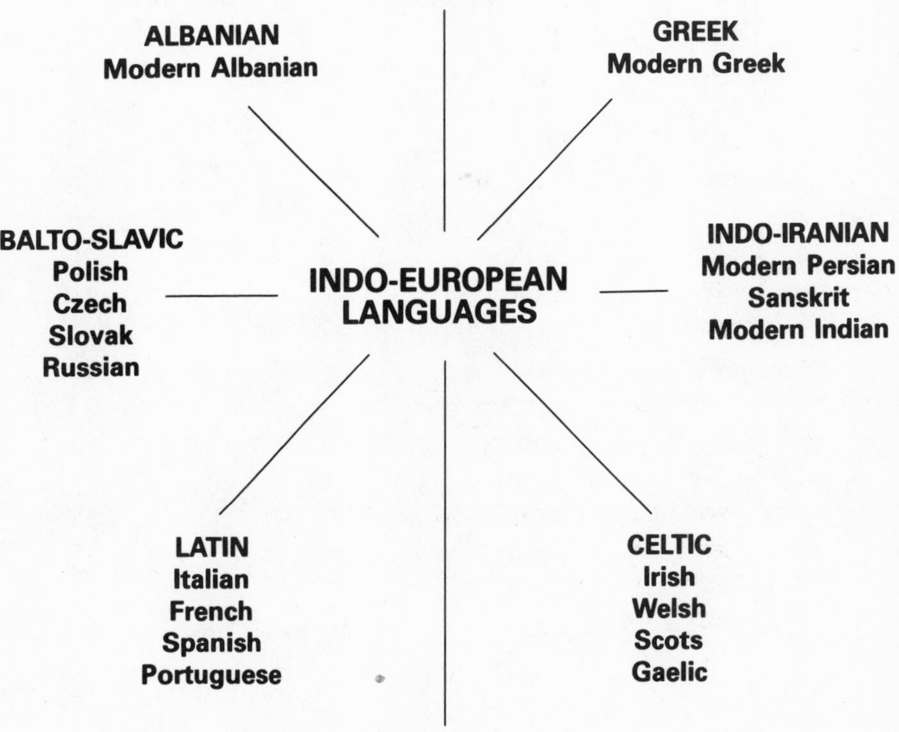
GERMANIC
English
Norwegian
Swedish
Danish
Dutch
German
ALBANIAN
Modern Albanian
GREEK
Modern Greek
BALTO-SLAVIC
Polish
Czech
Slovak
Russian
INDO-EUROPEAN
LANGUAGES
INDO-IRANIAN
Modern Persian
Sanskrit
Modern Indian
LATIN
Italian
French
Spanish
Portuguese
CELTIC
Irish
Welsh
Scots
Gaelic
ARMENIAN
Modern Armenian